Perfectly Loved:

Knowing Love on God's Terms

RHANA A. GITTENS

PERFECTLY LOVED: KNOWING LOVE ON GOD'S TERMS
Copyright © 2014 by Rhana A. Gittens
All rights reserved.

Published by:
NyreePress Literary Group
P.O. Box 164882
Fort Worth, TX 76161
www.nyreepress.com

All rights reserved. No part of this book may be used or reproduced by any means, graphic, electronic, or mechanical, including photocopying, recording, taping or by any information storage retrieval system without the written permission of the publisher. Copying this book is both illegal and unethical.

Scripture quotations marked (NLT) are taken from the Holy Bible, New Living Translation, copyright © 1996, 2004, 2007 by Tyndale House Foundation. Used by permission of Tyndale House Publishers, Inc., Carol Stream, Illinois 60188. All rights reserved.

THE HOLY BIBLE, NEW INTERNATIONAL VERSION®, NIV® Copyright © 1973, 1978, 1984, 2011 by Biblica, Inc.® Used by permission. All rights reserved worldwide.

Scripture taken from *The Message*. Copyright © 1993, 1994, 1995, 1996, 2000, 2001, 2002. Used by permission of NavPress Publishing Group

Scripture taken from the New King James Version®. Copyright © 1982 by Thomas Nelson, Inc. Used by permission. All rights reserved."

ISBN print: 978-0-9906662-3-3
Library of Congress Control Number: 2014954293
Category: Christian Living / Inspirational
Cover Photographer: Radim Schreiber

Printed in the United States of America

Dedication

Dedicated to Kevin and Linda Gittens -
My parents who were the first to share God's love with me.

And in loving memory of
Dorothy Jones and Robert Nolan
May their love for family always be remembered and cherished.

Contents

Dedication		3
Introduction		5
Chapter One –	LOVE IS INTERNAL AND ETERNAL	13
Chapter Two –	GOD'S LOVE FOR US	27
Chapter Three –	SHARING GOD'S LOVE TO OTHERS	38
Chapter Four –	THE GIFT OF LOVE	48
Chapter Five –	LOVE EXPELS FEAR	59
Chapter Six –	LOVE THROUGH ADVERSITY	81
Chapter Seven –	LOVING YOURSELF	99
Chapter Eight –	LOVE IN FAMILY	123
Chapter Nine –	LOVE IN FRIENDSHIP	140
Chapter Ten –	LOVE FORGIVES	158
Chapter Eleven –	LOVE SERVES	174
Chapter Twelve –	LOVING OTHERS TO CHRIST	187
Conclusion		204
Bibliography		205

Introduction

> *" 'You must love the Lord your God with all your heart, all your soul, and all your mind.' This is the first and greatest commandment. A second is equally important: 'Love your neighbor as yourself.' The entire law and all the demands of the prophets are based on these two commandments."*
>
> *– Matthew 22: 37-40*

All the law and the commandments are fulfilled in love. However, if we do not understand what love is, how can we fulfill the law? Walking in obedience to God isn't just following a handbook of 'do's' and 'don'ts'. On the contrary, obeying God starts with love. And love starts with understanding how God defined it.

Before I began my walk with Christ, and for some time after, I looked to define love through the dictionary, movies, romantic novels, and man-made concepts. As a teen, I was convinced that I knew what love was when I saw the movie *Love and Basketball* with Omar Epps and Sanaa Lathan. Surely my husband and I were going to meet as kids and fall in love over a game of Chinese Checkers (because I can't play basketball), and we would know it was love when I said, "I'll play you," and he would respond, "For what?" and I would declare, "For your heart." That was the epitome of the perfect love story, and nothing could keep me from believing that that would definitely be my life. That is, until I left elementary school…and middle school…and even high school with no "sweetheart."

My love matured a little in college. By college, I couldn't play childish games like basketball. My love would withstand the test of time like in *The Notebook*. Somehow I was going to meet this amazing guy on campus, and he was going to go off to war. But if he didn't go to the war, he would be secluded from society by some other means, like studying for a chemical engineering exam or pledging a fraternity. And during his seclusion, he would write me a letter (or "poke" me on Facebook) every single day, and we would chronicle our love in a journal (or change our Facebook statuses to "In a Complicated Relationship"). But I left college with no college sweetheart.

During my senior year of college and a few more maturing years after, I finally figured out what I was missing. I could not learn what love was through a man. I could not fulfill my lack of love with a man. And I could not read man-made books, watch man-made romantic comedies, or flirt with the Urban Dictionary to determine what love was. I realized that I could not go to man to define a word that was created by and first defined by God. I had to go to the inventor Himself—the Father, the Spirit, and the Son. It would take all three to learn this love stuff.

I began writing this book in May 2012. I was going through a rough season in my life where my spirit was unable to rest and I was nowhere near content with life. I had graduated college two years prior, and although I had a steady job, I was not living my dream. I was ready to leave the college town of Gainesville, Florida, but had been applying to jobs for four months and wasn't getting any responses. I felt claustrophobic from being in a small city. I saw the entire world growing and moving, while I was just existing. The friendships I had based my Gainesville existence on were crumbling beneath my feet. People were growing apart and growing in different directions, and there was no way to hold on to them. My day-to-day life became hard to bear without the laughter and companionship of my closest friends nearby.

Within just a three-month span, I had been hurt by three men. I had fantasized (as girls often do) my life with one guy, only to find out he had a baby and was getting married. Then another potential suitor came into my life proclaiming that he was ready to propose to me and not have sex until marriage. He stood for all the things I thought I wanted or needed at the time to complete my wish list, but in a flash he decided for whatever reason that he needed time to be single (six months later I found out that he was engaged and expecting). In this very short span of time in early 2012, my father and I had an argument, partially due to my own immaturity in handling the situation, and we went without speaking to each other for three weeks.

I was saved and committed to God at the time and was truly walking the walk (at least I thought I was). For a long time I had been growing and maturing at a fast pace in my relationship with God, but during the first five months of 2012 I felt like I was just going through the motions with God. I had a routine: Bible study on Wednesday, college and young adult ministry events on Friday and Saturday, and church service on Sunday. But I wanted more. Unfortunately, I wasn't pushing for more of Him. I was yearning more for worldly successes than the success that comes with knowing and understanding God's love. When I finally couldn't take my seemingly stagnant existence anymore, I broke down. I ran away from life for three days and went to Tampa to lie on my brother and sister-in-law's couch and play with my one-year-old niece. I called my mom and dad, and I begged for love. I ran back to the three people on this earth that I thought loved me first—my mom, dad, and brother. But while I sat on their couch and watched my niece waddle around the living room in all her innocence, I thought about how much I loved her. I said to her, "I love you because right now at this age you are the only person that can't do a single thing to hurt me." But then God shined a light on me as if I were crazy. He said to me, "What are you talking about, girl? I AM the one who would never hurt you. I AM the one you run to. I AM the first one to have ever loved you." And after that moment, I just started writing and researching in the Bible all the verses that declared God's love for me. I didn't completely understand the fullness of God's love at this point, but I knew that God was about to show Himself to me in an amazing way, and I knew that what I was writing would become a book. I also knew that everything that had happened prior to that day was strategically planned in order to bring me to a place of brokenness, to hear from God, and to write His book—*Perfectly Loved*.

In my eyes, *Perfectly Loved* will always be God's book. It was never my idea or thought to begin with. It has always been His. I give Him all the glory for this book. It is only in and through the Holy Spirit that it has been written. However, if there are any errors in this book, those are all mine. I take credit for the errors, and I give God the glory for the one or one million people who will know God's love better just from reading these pages. If just one person's life is changed by its pages, then every page was worth it.

Perfectly Loved is a testimonial, but it is not about me or a biography of my life. Each chapter has testimonies and anecdotes of my own life lessons. It also includes testimonies from readers like you under sections called "My Story." These testimonies do not mean that your walk with God will be the same, but they are included so that you know that you do not walk alone in your faith or in your struggles. These testimonies declare God's love and reveal His love story to all of us. Note that some of the "My Story" names have been altered for the protection of the story teller.

Perfectly Loved is not a how-to-be-a-good-single-Christian, how-to-get-married-to-a-Christian, or how-to-find-love-with-a-good-Christian-man-or-woman manual. This book is all about the one love relationship that defines the beginning and the end of our lives. This book is about our vertical love relationship with God. As we discuss that vertical relationship, we will make a perpendicular line with our horizontal relationships with other people. I visualize the vertical and horizontal relationships of love like a waterfall.

As God's love pores down like a rushing waterfall into us, we disperse that love to the people around us causing fruit and plants to grow and seeds to be nourished within them. Those horizontal relationships are the base of our vertical relationship with God. Through them we show God's love and share God's love and declare our understanding and faith in His love.

Perfectly Loved is an interactive book. Take out your pens and a journal. You will not just read this book, but you will fill in the blanks of its pages with your own stories. Questions and exercises are included in the book throughout the chapters to supplement your reading. Unless otherwise noted, all Bible verses are written in New Living Translation.

I pray that as you read these pages, your heart will be opened and your mind be freed. I pray that you are able to see God speak what He wants you to hear and that you will apply the lessons to your life. Share this book with others not only by passing it along but by truly exemplifying God's love as you write the pages of your own book through your life with Christ.

Love Always,

Rhana A. Gittens

Chapter One
LOVE IS INTERNAL AND ETERNAL

Study Verse -- *"Therefore we do not lose heart. Even though the outward man is perishing, the inward man is renewed day by day. For our light affliction, which is but for a moment is working for us a far more exceeding and eternal weight of glory, while we do not look at the things which are seen, but at the things which are not seen. For the things which are seen are temporary, but the things which are not seen are eternal."* - 2 Corinthians 4:16-18 (NKJV)

When I Googled, "Why we are here?" it came up with 970,000,000 results. Various philosophers, religions, psychologists, and artists attempt to answer this question that baffles the human race. At some point of deep and contemplative thought of our human lives we all eventually ask the question "Why are we here?" For some it's just a passing thought and for others it causes a full exploration of meaning that may lead to infinite answers.

According to Sigmund Freud our lives are meant to reach a compromise between our instincts and societal expectations. The Yoga philosophy states that we are to devote our lives to attain self-realization and absolute freedom. In Hamlet, Shakespeare poetically writes "All that lives must die, passing through nature to eternity." And according to Groundhog Day we are here to live the same day, over and over again, until we get it right[1]. With some imaginative thought others have also claimed that we are a part of someone else's dream or possibly we are just in a big video game that someone is playing.

I personally think Glinda, the Good Witch of the North, got it right in *The Wizard of Oz*. Dorothy traveled throughout Oz to find the Wizard to get her home. The Wizard turned out to be a fraud. But what Dorothy didn't realize is that she didn't need that wizard to get her home. She had the power to get home within her the entire time. From *The Wizard of Oz* we learn that instead of looking outward to answer "why", we should be looking inward.

The gift of living two thousand years after Christ is that we have a complete book of everything God wants us to know about Him and about ourselves. The Bible gives us all the information that is necessary for us to live life on earth. Of course there is a lot more to know and understand about God. However, God feeds us with just enough to be successful in our current state. People keep asking the "why?" questions because they don't believe the Bible is all of it; they don't believe the Bible is true, or they don't believe that there is life after our mere one hundred years on earth. I am not here to argue with you about the truth of the Bible. I am here to declare its truth and affirm the ultimate and only answer to "Why?"—LOVE!

Paul writes in 1 Corinthians 13:1-3, 12-13, "If I could speak all the languages of earth and of angels, but didn't love others, I would only be a noisy gong or a clanging cymbal. If I had the gift of prophecy, and if I understood all of God's secret plans and possessed all knowledge, and if I had such faith that I could move mountains, but didn't love others, I would be nothing. If I gave everything I have to the poor and even sacrificed my body, I could boast about it, but if I didn't love others, I would have gained nothing ... Now we see things imperfectly, like puzzling reflections in a mirror, but when we see Jesus face-to-face we will see everything with perfect clarity. All that I know now is partial and incomplete, but when I see Jesus I will know everything completely, just as God now knows me completely. Three things will last forever—faith, hope, and love—and the greatest of these is love."

Right now we live life with a partial view of its fullness. If we knew everything, we would likely mess up everything. We have to be spoon-fed, because too much would kill us. Even Moses couldn't take seeing all of God. He would have died by seeing more than just His backside (Exodus 33:18-23). God and the knowledge of everything is too much for us to handle as humans, nor is it necessary for our purpose. We are able to live out our purpose with the information that God has given us. God, through His almighty being, brought us to earth in order to exemplify the ultimate part of who He is—LOVE!

Love is everything. Love is God, and love is why we live. If we don't completely understand it, hold on to it, and embody it, we will not live in the fullness that God called us to.

Perfectly Loved: Knowing Love on God's Terms

So how does "love" answer "why"? Well, the first step in understanding Agape love is to look inward. You have to recognize the eternal part of your being. Love is born out of the eternal, everlasting parts of ourselves. In order for you to recognize the eternal birthplace of love, you must see yourself in the fullness of your three parts: your spirit, your soul, and your flesh. As humans we live eternally as a spirit, we have a soul, and we dwell in a body. Your spirit is your innermost man that is conscious to God and spiritual beings. Your soul houses your mind, emotions, conscience, will, and thought processes. Your flesh is your connection to the world. Your flesh is "what" you are. Your soul defines "how" you do what you do. But your spirit answers "why" you do it. Your spirit affects the motivation for all of your actions. Even after your body dies, your spirit is still alive. Your spirit lives to go to heaven or hell.

SPIRIT - answers "Why"

SOUL - answers "How"

FLESH - answers "What"

Rhana A. Gittens

It is extremely important to make a clear distinction between your body and your spirit. Your spirit is connected to God, while your flesh connects you to the world. God is unseen; the world is visible. God is eternal, while the world is temporary. When we speak of eternal aspects of God's character, we are referring to spiritual things. The flesh is temporary and will die, but things of the spirit will never pass away.

Love comes from the spirit (the inward man) where all things are eternal. God lives within our spirit, and love is birthed from God's location within our three-part being. When love is in your spirit, the motivating factor for "what" you do is love. Love becomes your "why". Because the birthplace of love is from the location of God within us, the ultimate goal of life is to love others and love God to bring pleasure and glory to God. Our God is so glorious that things that bring Him pleasure last forever. If it doesn't last forever, it is not good enough for God.

LOVE IS...	LOVE IS NOT...
• patient	• rude
• kind	• self-seeking
• rejoicing in the truth	• jealous
• a bearer of all things	• proud
• faithful	• boastful
• hopeful	• easily provoked
• enduring all things	• evil
	• rejoicing in injustice
	• able to fail

Let's break down how God defines love further. Although I had heard 1 Corinthians 13 and acknowledged it as a definition of love, it wasn't until I tore apart its pieces that it truly came to life for me. At first, 1 Corinthians 13 was only good for me when it came to romantic relationships. However, these verses were not written about romance. The verses of 1 Corinthians 13 declare the one law that God has forced us to have in every relationship, including relationships with ourselves, God, bosses, lawyers, bankers, enemies, friends, family, and criminals. Unconditional and eternal, God's love is for all.

In 1 Corinthians 13, Paul lists all the things love is and the things love is not. All the adjectives and verbs that Paul uses to describe what love is or does are eternal. Paul states love is <u>patient</u>, is <u>kind</u>, is <u>faithful</u> <u>rejoices</u> in the <u>truth</u>, bears <u>all</u> things, <u>hopes</u> <u>all</u> things, and <u>endures</u> <u>all</u> things. All the single underlined words are articles that describe the characteristics of love as having no ending. All the double underlined words are actions of the spirit to show love in action. Love is an action, not a feeling. Other versions of this same chapter use the phrase "all things" to describe each of the characteristics of love. "All things" covers everything. We can believe, hope, and bear *some* things on our own, but it takes God, who is love Himself, to believe, hope, and bear "all things".

For instance, love rejoices in truth. In this regard, love celebrates the truth about people and events. Love refuses to set up deceit against others or falsehoods about events. Furthermore, if you endure and bear all things, you carry or hold on to the burdens of all people and all matters that are true. Therefore, acting in eternal love will keep you from losing hope and quitting on people and things that you believe in.

Rhana A. Gittens

The actions of an eternal love are based in fellowship and relationship with others, yourself, and God. Despite your feelings about a matter or a person, you can express love through your spirit and have it work out in your actions. Your flesh alone will create emotions that cause you to act out. However, the issue with acting on emotions is that emotions are temporary.

God is very specific in 1 Corinthians 13 in describing the temporary emotional states that are in no way shape or form love. Paul states love is not <u>rude</u>, is not <u>self-seeking</u>, is not <u>jealous</u>, is not <u>proud</u>, is not <u>boastful</u>, is not easily <u>provoked</u>, is not <u>evil</u>, does not rejoice in <u>lies</u>, and does not <u>fail</u>. To be unruly, envious, boastful, or easily angered are all temporary emotions. We regret our actions when they are based out of emotions, because once the emotion has left us, we have a change of heart in the way we should have handled the situation. However, when the motivation for your actions comes from your spirit as eternal love, your heart will never change in regards to how you handled the situation. There are no regrets when you act in love.

For example, to be envious of someone is to have such jealousy of what they have and their blessings that you would steal it from them, pray against them having it, or set up a way to keep them from having it. You may feel as though the other person does not deserve what they have garnered. However, if you were successful in getting what they have, your happiness would be short-lived, and in a matter of time you would be yearning for something else. Furthermore, love does not boast. If you parade yourself around and show off your blessings in vanity to others, you are also seeking a temporary form of pleasure that will not leave you content. Failure, envy, evil, and vanity are all temporary and based on or caused by lustful cravings for worldly attributes.

When our love does not have an ultimate motive of bringing pleasure and glory to God, it becomes subject to our ulterior motives. Our ulterior motives display themselves through lusts for pleasure, image, and status. These motivations come from love of the world and personal desires. When we are "loving" someone or something, we have to question our inner selves and ask, "Is my love for _____ (fill-in-the-blank) based on my personal need for pleasure, image, or a status in my life?"

The Bible states in 1 John 2:15-17 (NIV), "Do not love the world or anything in the world. If anyone loves the world, the love of the Father is not in him. For everything in the world—the cravings of sinful man (pleasure), the lust of the eyes (image), and the boasting of what he has and does (status)—comes not from the Father but from the world. The world and its desires pass away, but the man who does the will of God lives forever."

Thereby, all sin is from these three temptations that result from love of the world—the lust of the flesh (pleasure), the lust of the eyes (image), and the pride of life (status). Lust is a passionate and overwhelming desire or craving for something or someone. Lust is not just the people we associate with, the places we go, or the activities we do. Rather, it is the internal motivating factors that cause us to choose to associate with a specific group of people, go to specific locations, or join in specific actions.

Rhana A. Gittens

The human motivation for pleasure reveals itself in a craving for things that provide physical satisfaction and enjoyment. We may find temporary pleasure in money, power, or connection with other people. These cravings can lead to struggles with loneliness, depression, pornography, sexual immorality, alcoholism, and drug addictions.

Furthermore, when we are motivated by a sense of image, we are thinking of love from a materialistic stand point, concerned with beauty and accumulating things. Not only are we looking toward the image of the person or thing we are lusting for but also the image of ourselves when we have or don't have the item that we have set our sights on. When you purchase a new phone simply because everyone else has it, you may be thinking about the image or the perception people will have of you when they see you with it. When you walk away from a great guy or gal because he or she isn't a cute enough arm accessory, you are behaving in a lust for image.

Finally, when we are motivated to love based on what it can do for us, we are thinking based on the pride of life. The pride of life can be extremely subtle, but it is exemplified by a need for achievement and possessions. It may even be realized in a need for power, importance, and status. For example, the world makes it feel shameful for you to be single, so we often get into relationships simply to have the "in a relationship" status. We join organizations, take jobs, and spend money we don't have in order to portray a status. Statuses are extremely temporary (ask the 5,000 people who changed their status to "single" today on Facebook.

Perfectly Loved: Knowing Love on God's Terms

Then consult the 10,000 Facebook followers that "liked" there "single" status). When we are motivated by our pride, we find ourselves addicted to a temporary opportunity and holding on to things that aren't good for us or things we don't really even want.

When everything else is gone away and the temporariness of it all becomes all too familiar, you finally see that love was not in your pleasures, image, or status. Those motivations are here in this life, but they don't go with you to the grave. However, God's love is unconditional, and it is with you eternally. Love is best characterized by abiding fellowship with God and it is a never-ending relationship with oneself, others, and God. When you know that pleasure, image, and status are temporary in this world, would you have courage to deny yourself these things for God's eternal love?

Our study scripture for this chapter states that "we do not look at things which are seen, but at the things which are not seen. For the things which are seen are temporary, but the things which are not seen are eternal" (2 Corinthians 4:16-18, NKJV). This may seem like a weird verse to describe love, but on the contrary, it describes love perfectly. Love is not something we can see, taste, touch, hear, or smell. It is not in the brand-new home you bought for your family, promotions on the job, or even the exhilaration of sex. Love is not even the feeling of a hug from the person sitting next to you in church. Those big church hugs feel really good, but love isn't the hug itself; rather, it is the unseen part of that person. It dwells internally. Love is in their spirit. People describe sex as "making love," but it is only truly "making love" if you actually love that person unconditionally. Otherwise, it is just sex.

Because we know we can't feel love from our five senses, it is clear that in order to truly feel and give love, we have to do it from the inner most part of us: our spirit. When we love people from our spirit man, we can love people we don't really like. "Liking" someone comes from your soul. "Liking" someone is your mind's thoughts about that person and what they have done; loving someone is about who they are spiritually. Who someone is spiritually is not based on what they have done but what God can do through them and how God defines them. Love causes you to believe God's truth about them and hope for the best of God to shine through them. That's how we can love a rapist. We may not "like" a rapist, because our minds tell us that everything they did was wrong and hurtful; but our spirits tell us that God can redeem them through His loving power, make them new, and bring them back to be more like Him.

All people were originally created to be in the image of God, and we have been separated from that image. The good news is that loving through the spirit gives you the constant reminder that God can redeem anyone back to Him. So you love people not because of what they have done but who they are and can be with Christ. Who they are in Christ is eternal; they just have to live through their spirit and not their flesh in order to get back to what God created them for.

Dorothy was searching for the meaning of her life. She was running away from her family and looking for more. But when

Perfectly Loved: Knowing Love on God's Terms

Dorothy reached the end of her journey and she found out the answer was always within her. She states the famous line "there is no place like home"[2]. At home she finds the true unconditional love that is the defining meaning of life. Within our spirits we will find home and the answer to "why". And when God indwells with you as the master of your spirit, your "why" is love.

Think About It

1. **If you could do, be, and have anything you want (limitless) in this lifetime, what would it be?**

   _____
   _____
   _____
   _____

2. **What are your motivating factors for achieving or receiving this dream? List them.**

   _____
   _____
   _____
   _____
   _____

3. **Review your list. Which of your motivating factors are temporary pleasures, image, or status? List them.**

Rhana A. Gittens

_____

_____

4. Which of your motivating factors are eternal? (refer to 1 Corinthians 13)

_____

_____

5. If you took away all of the temporary factors that motivate this dream, would your dream change? If so, how would it change?

_____

_____

_____

_____

MY STORY – JAMIL

I played football in high school, and football is a macho sport. You have this mind-set of going into battle when you run on that field. But on the other end, you know that you could get injured, and you could lose the battle. In order to play that game and feel secure you have to have faith in something. When I played, I never felt secure.

One of my teammates would pray in the huddle. He would say, "Fear no man but God" and start the Lord's Prayer. I would try to call on those prayers myself, but it never seemed to work for

Perfectly Loved: Knowing Love on God's Terms

me. I just felt empty. Maybe my other teammates felt like they had someone with them on the field, but I felt alone. That was before I was saved by Christ. That's when I was Muslim. Back then, I didn't really feel God's presence. I was scared of a lot of things. But God's unconditional love saved me. Now, I'm not scared. When I am faced with difficult situations, I call on God, and I feel like He is there. He gives me hope. He gives me love.

These days, for me winning the battle is more than a football game. It's being a good husband, raising my daughter, loving others, and growing in my career. Before I had Christ, I felt like I was fighting on my own and everything I got seemed temporary. But now that I have Him, I know that when His love blesses me it is permanent. My licenses and degrees came through a lot of sacrifice, hard times, crying, and struggle. I did not always think I was going to make it, but once I achieved it, and I knew God's love had pushed me through, I knew no one could ever take it away. That's the difference between doing things through the power of man and the power of God. What God blesses can never be taken away by man.

That's what God's love is to me. It's pure. It's unconditional. It's permanent. No matter what I do, His love never goes away. I can go into any battle now, and I can win.

Rhana A. Gittens

Chapter Two
God's Love for Us

Study Verse - *"For this is the covenant that I will make with the house of Israel after those days, says the Lord; I will put my laws into their mind and write them on their hearts; and I will be their God, and they shall be my people." Hebrews 8:10-13 (NKJV)*

God's love for us is so infinite and massive that a few words could never describe it in its entirety. What many people fail to understand is that love is not our capacity to show some miraculous emotion or action of charity to another. Very simply put in 1 John 4:10, "This is real love—not that we loved God, but that He loved us and sent His Son as a sacrifice to take away our sins." In knowing that truth, we should love others. This is where we begin to define love and how we can be transformed by it.

From the beginning of creation, God loved us without any special actions on our part. When He created Adam and Eve (Genesis 1-3), He wanted to be able to walk freely with Him. God made a promise (covenant) with the first man and woman that they could have everything in the Garden of Eden as long as they did not eat from the forbidden tree of the knowledge of good and evil. Unfortunately, Adam and Eve didn't keep the promise, and after eating from the tree they became conscious of their sin and covered their nakedness. Because they broke their covenant promise with God, He banished them from the garden, and their rights to see and be with God at all times were removed. But God always wanted to be reconciled with His creation again.

He created a covenant with Moses (Deuteronomy 28: 1-2) and presented the Ten Commandments (Exodus 20:1-22). The covenant with Moses was that if man fulfilled *all* of God's commandments, He would bless them. But man was unable to fulfill all of the commandments. Therefore, God told them to create an altar of sacrifices and that He would bless them based on their burnt offerings. God stressed that He wanted to be able to bless His people who He loved, but they could never keep their end of the bargain.

The Ten Commandments are also called "the Law," and the purpose of the law was to show man that He was too weak to be able to live in this world without God. The problem was not with the law but with man. The only thing that could redeem man and reconcile his relationship with God was love. And God's love for us was expressed through the ultimate sacrifice of Jesus Christ.

On that cross, Jesus had your name in mind. He envisioned you when he took those lashes. And that is love. Because He died for your sins, you do not have to live in guilt, shame, or regret. God wants you to live knowing you are His righteousness. Jesus's blood covers you. When God looks at you, He does not see your sin, but He sees His Son (Romans 4).

Having grown up Muslim, I was taught that God was making a list of all of my good deeds and all of my bad deeds. If my good deeds outweighed my bad deeds, I would go to heaven. However, when I came to believe in Jesus, I had to renew my mind to the knowledge that God was not keeping a running tally of my sins. Rather, Jesus died for my sins, and I am forgiven. He did the same for you.

The Apostle John writes, "If you believe in your heart and confess with your mouth that Jesus died and rose again on the third day you are saved" (1 John 3:16). You are forgiven, and you didn't have to do anything in order to get God's forgiveness, mercy, grace, or His love except believe. As humans, we have a hard time understanding that we can get something without giving something. We think that because we may be doing good things, serving our community, and paying tithes regularly that God then owes us His love. But God loved you when you weren't doing any of that stuff. He loved you while you were in your sin. He blessed you in the midst of your sin. He comforted you from a broken heart when getting a broken heart was caused because you stepped out on God. Love is that God loved us so much that even when we didn't love Him, "He gave…"

For God, love was never defined by our love for Him. We turn our backs on Him the moment we walk out the church on Sunday. So if He was counting on us to have some unconditional,

Perfectly Loved: Knowing Love on God's Terms

eternal love for Him in order for Him to exist, then He would be in desperate need of a respirator right now.

When babies are first born, and even at the moment we learn that a baby is coming, we grow in unconditional love for them. We love our newborn baby because he or she is ours. We love our baby because we know that this baby is totally dependent on us for their life and survival. The only thing we hope to get in return from our children is love. That is exactly how God views us.

My mom always tells me that when I was a little girl, I would drive her nuts calling, "Mommy, Mommy, Mommy," over and over in the house. As soon as she said, "What, Rhana?" I would respond, "I love you." It was bothersome then, but when I got to my teenage years and stopped saying, "I love you, Mommy," all she wanted to hear was, "I love you, Mommy." In the same way, God feels this unconditional love for us. He doesn't ask for anything in return, but He loves to hear us praise Him by saying, "I love you." If you haven't told Him "I love you" in a while, I'm sure He probably misses hearing it just like the parents of teenagers.

After Jesus died and was resurrected, God created a new covenant with His people. This new covenant is described in Hebrews 8:10-13. "This is the covenant that I will make with the house of Israel after those days, says the Lord; I will put my laws in their minds and I will write them on their hearts; I will be their God, and they will be my people."

Love is fulfilled when you genuinely believe in the love God has for you. When you believe, God will change your heart, imprint His laws on it, and give you His Spirit so that you can walk out in His eternal love.

If this is true, why are there so many Christians who profess salvation but lack love? Christians don't show kindness to their neighbor. Christians backstab just like non-believers. Christians are in the world hurting others just like they did before they confessed their belief. This occurs because there is a difference between realizing the truth and being convicted by the truth. When you realize the truth that Jesus died for your sins, you are only recognizing it as a fact that even the devil knows (James 2:19). But when you are convicted by this truth, your heart is changed in order to elicit a behavioral transformation. Though believers confess that they believe God died for them, it is not until they truly are convicted by God's love for them that the Holy Spirit can renew their mind.

The result of conviction is commitment to truth. In that commitment you do all you can to display that truth. When you believe in God's love for you to the point of conviction, your actions will work toward exemplifying that certainty by obeying Him. Even when you mess up, you will get back up and keep trying harder to show to the world that God's love is evident through your own life. God doesn't just want you to know His love, but He wants His love to elicit a behavioral change so that it is unmistakable that you believe in His love. When you know your heavenly Father's love for you, there are things you will stop doing simply because you know you are a reflection of Him, and you don't want Him to ever be disappointed in you.

Perfectly Loved: Knowing Love on God's Terms

Yes, we can say quickly, "I know Jesus died for me on Calvary." But there comes a point in every Christian's life that they wake up and realize, "Oh my, God loves me. He loves me and I don't know why." It happened to me. God suddenly began to overwhelm me with blessings and pulled me out of bad situations that I was happily (but blindly) putting myself into. Everything that I thought could go wrong... didn't. He kept protecting me despite all of my shortcomings. That is God's love. There should come a day in every Christian's life when they wake up and are strongly convicted by the love of God. God will bless some people so much that they fall to their knees in realization of this underserved love. He may bless until it hurts. God might put other people through hard times, tests, and trials until they fall to their knees in realization that only God's love is unconditionally able to save. Regardless of how the conviction of God's love hits, it *will* hit. There will be a moment when you ask Him, "God, why do you continue to bless me when I suck?" When that moment comes in your life, you are finally starting to understand and comprehend the magnitude of God's love. In that moment He will simply whisper, "Because I love you."

Love is not that we love but that He loves. His Spirit gives us the ability to love as He does. With a clear conscience, free of guilt, we can ask God to make us better at loving, and He will grant our request.

In 1 John 4:17, the Apostle John writes, "As we live in God, our love *grows* more perfect." If your love is expected to grow more perfect, then it is not expected to be complete the moment that you confess your belief in salvation. Therefore, you should not feel guilty when you realize your love is not perfect or you have made more lovely mistakes than lovely actions. You will be strengthened by the Word of God the closer you grow in God's love. God will perfect our love.

Now I must place this disclaimer. Many will begin to read this and quickly think that this is an "out" in following the Ten Commandments. Some may be thinking, "God will forgive me, and I shouldn't feel guilt, so I can do what I want." But that is not the case at all. The purpose of Jesus's death was for us to realize that the only way to fulfill the Ten Commandments is through love. Once you realize His love and everlasting grace are abounding in you, you're going to want to love others and be obedient to all of God's commandments. David says in Psalm 37:4, "Delight yourself in the Lord, and He will give you your heart's desires." This verse means that God will literally change your old worldly desires and give you new ones that are in line with God's purpose for your life. Therefore, it is no longer by your own ability that you can be obedient to God. Now it is God's ability to change your heart as you seek Him that allows you to fulfill the Law and love others as He loves you.

The knowledge of these simple truths about God's love for us helps us deepen our understanding of love and how to show it and share it with others. It helps us understand how God works and why love came through Jesus Christ in order to fulfill the Law. Through our belief in our savior, we can live as the righteous seed of God.

Perfectly Loved: Knowing Love on God's Terms

Think About It

1. Make a list of up to 5 "good" things you did within the last 48 hours.

   a. _____
   b. _____
   c. _____
   d. _____
   e. _____

2. Make a list of up to 5 "bad" things or sins you committed within the last 48 hours.

   a. _____
   b. _____
   c. _____
   d. _____
   e. _____

3. Make a list of all the blessings (big or small) God bestowed upon you within the last 48 hours.

   a. _____
   b. _____
   c. _____

Rhana A. Gittens

    d. _____

    e. _____

4. **Do you need more space?**

    a. _____

    b. _____

    c. _____

    d. _____

    e. _____

5. **What did you do today to deserve those blessings?**

_____

_____

6. **Is there anything to praise God for? If so, what is it?**

_____

_____

MY STORY – RYAN

When I think of loving someone so much that you give up your life for them, I think of my mother. She raised me by herself, and everything she did revolved around me. As a child, I didn't appreciate it; but as I've grown older, I realize that she showed me what love is.

Perfectly Loved: Knowing Love on God's Terms

I don't feel indebted to her because I know she gave me all of that freely, unconditionally. When I think of debt, I think of an expectation from the giver to get something in return. But I know my mother would love me regardless. Nonetheless, I feel like she deserves much more than what I have given her. A debt is something you can pay off, but I don't know if I could ever pay her back for all the love she has shown me.

My mother's love for me reminds me of God's love for me. I don't think my human mind can fully comprehend God's love. If God's love had a debt on it, I could never pay it back. He gave His Son to die for me, and I did nothing to deserve it. I didn't do anything to deserve my mother's love either.

If my mom took her love away from me, I would be pretty upset. While on the other hand, it's hard for me to miss having a father's love because I never experienced it. When I think of my experiences of love, I realize why it is so difficult to explain God's love to nonbelievers: they can't miss what they don't know.

As a believer, the best thing I can do is show the love that the nonbeliever has never felt. I have to imitate Christ. Christ *is* love. Love isn't a verb for God. Rather, God is the definition of love. Through the power of the Holy Spirit, I can show God's love to others.

I once had a girl I liked break up with me to date one of my best friends. She basically said to me, "Sorry, I'm in love with someone else, but we can still be friends." My heart was broken, but instead of beating up my friend or calling the girl out of her name, I told her that I would always be her friend. That's one of the best examples I can think of where the love I showed for someone paralleled God's love for me. When I think about it, a lot of my actions probably say to God, "Sorry, I'm in love with someone else, but we can still be friends." When I put my career and other people before Him, He doesn't disown me. Rather, He simply replies, "Okay, I still love you. I'll be here when you need me." That's love. God's love for me never changes. I change. But God's love is always there. I have to show that to others. Sometimes people don't see things until they actually see it. I guess that means that I have to show it.

Chapter Three

Sharing God's Love to Others

Study Verse – *"This is real love — not that we loved God, but that he loved us and sent his Son as a sacrifice to take away our sins."* 1 John 4:10

A broken heart makes you want to just grab your chest, go beneath your rib cage wall, and hug your heart in order to sooth its pain. When it's really bad, you want to clutch your heart and completely rip it out in hopes that the absence of a heart would cause the pain of its brokenness to disappear. It hits so deep that you truly feel like you will just die. But then you wake the next morning in realization that you are living, and you are living without the person that you thought you couldn't live without. Unfortunately, if not taken care of, a broken heart can fester into a life of unforgiveness and a life devoid of love.

One day after work, I was feverishly texting an old friend that I was having a very hard time forgiving. In my mind, he had turned his back on me when I was willing to give up my back, front, and side for him. In the last text he sent me before I walked out the office, he said the famous line that I've heard from far too many guys, "I've been hurt before, and I don't know how to love people anymore." Basically, he was trying to tell me that he had had that intense level of broken-heartedness where he reached in his heart and just pulled it out completely, and now there was an icebox where his heart used to be. Our conversation could have turned out to be long and drawn out. I could have explained all the things he put me through and how much he hurt me. But for once I decided to end it. Or rather, the Spirit told me to end it, and I simply texted him back, "I forgive you."

As I drove home, I contemplated why that moment was so important. I thought, *Well maybe* me *freely forgiving* him *would help him to forgive the person who hurt him.* I considered all the noble things I could do to show him how to love again. But the Spirit again stopped me and explained that the glory needed to be God's and not my own.

When I got home, I got in bed to take a nap, but the Spirit would not let me rest. Before I knew it, I was repeating 1 John 4:10 over and over. "Love is not that we love God, but that He loves us." It just kept repeating in my head, and I finally understood its full meaning. I was called to forgive him, not because he loved me or deserved forgiveness, but because I loved him and was called to set him free so that he could one day put his heart back in the place of that icebox.

Maybe that explanation for forgiveness doesn't mean much to you now, but in the understanding of 1 John 4:10 we not only learn why God loves us but why we are called to love others.

Perfectly Loved: Knowing Love on God's Terms

In order to understand our godly relationship with others, we can change a few of the words of the study verse for this chapter and make it personal.

"Love is not that people love me, but that I love them and give up my life for my brother and sister."

Let's take it further. Put your name in it.

"Love is not that people love _____, but that _____ loves people and gives up _____'s life for _____'s brothers and sisters."

Wow, that's even harder to grasp, isn't it? Do I really have to love people who don't love me? Who don't do anything for me? Even beyond that, do I have to give up my life for these jokers who I don't even like? Yes, yes, and yes. And I preface this with saying that I know this isn't easy. But it isn't easy because we walk in our worldly flesh and don't let the Spirit take over. The world tells us to be vindictive, rebellious, and vengeful. But "I will take revenge. I will pay them back," says the Lord (Hebrews 10:30).

I used to watch a lot of reality TV shows. A few of my old addictions were *Love and Hip Hop*, *Real Housewives of Atlanta*, and so and so's Family Chronicles. You name it; I watched it. I stopped watching them as much because I realize that every time I watched that madness, I was letting these vindictive, rebellious, and vengeful spirits seep into my own mind. And what a man "thinks in his heart so is he" (Proverbs 23:7 NKJV). But the revelation that comes out of watching these shows is that the world is vindictive, rebellious, and vengeful. If you stole my chicken, I must surely have to steal your boyfriend. Ridiculous, right? But this is what is on the hearts of man. This is how we treat each other. We don't know love by God's standards. All we know is what the Bible defines as lust (Galatians 5:16).

It is important for Christians to have an understanding of how the world is, because it will help you discern between spiritual love and lust of the flesh. Your Spirit will never tell you to get revenge when someone hurts you. Your Spirit will never tell you to lie your way to be the V.P. of Joe Bank. Your Spirit will never tell you to leave your friend when they can't give you anything in return.

Your Spirit will tell you to forgive that one person seven hundred times even when they may not ask for forgiveness. Your Spirit will tell you to wait on God to move you to the position that He has promised and prepared for you. Your Spirit will tell you to keep on giving, even when no one loves you back or provides anything in return for your love.

No, you may not like everyone. I'm sure God doesn't always like us. But like and love are two totally different things. Like is an emotional response. Love is something we have to consciously do. It is not an emotional feeling. Love is giving without expectation of return. It's a simple definition for a word that seems to cause so much trouble. And it's crazy that the word that God created in order to save our souls, fulfill the law, and create peace has become the hardest word for people to grasp. It's probably the most wrongly used word, but the word that is most necessary when used correctly. The problem is not the overuse of the word *love*. If it were up to God, we would use it at all times in our relationships. The problem is, we say the word but don't do any of the actions that come with its meaning. The problem is that we don't know what God wanted it to mean, because we don't give God the credit for the most amazing thing He ever created—LOVE!

You are called to love others, and you can love others. The Apostle John writes, "Let us continue to love one another, for love comes from God. Anyone who loves is a child of God and knows God. But anyone who does not love does not know God, for God is love" (1 John 4:7-8). Could you imagine being face-to-face with God but Him turning away from you and saying, "You did not love your brothers and sisters, so I do not know you"? I know just the thought of it is sickening to me. All of us in our cars singing, "I am a friend of God, He calls me friend." Then we turn around and curse out the man in front of us for driving too slow. What if you called out, "Lord! Lord!" and God responded, "I never knew you"? (Mathew 7: 21-23)

In 1 Peter 4:7-9 (NKJV), God says, "Most important of all, continue to show *fervent* love for each other, for love covers a multitude of sins." The definition of fervent is having or showing great warmth or intensity of spirit or feeling. God's word is saying that showing deep, spiritual love for each other covers your sins. This again takes us back to the key scripture of *Perfectly Loved*—Matthew 22:37-40—that all of the law is fulfilled in love. The sins of the law would not occur if we obeyed the command of love. Love is the opposition to all forms of sin. If you are committing a sin, you are showing a specific lack of love for someone or something. A sin can exemplify a lack of love for yourself, a family member, a neighbor, or even God. Every type of sin is an exhibition of a lack of love in some aspect of our lives. Through our mistakes and sins, we can determine where we are lacking and repent and pray that God mend our hearts.

When you understand God's love for you, there is no way you would commit adultery, fornicate, covet another's goods, cheat, or lie. God's love begins to change your heart so much that the desire to sin diminishes when you believe and earnestly seek to be closer to Him. The closer you get to perfecting your love, the more your heart will be set on the desires of God. Before He left the earth, Jesus informed us that God's desire is to spread His gospel to the entire world (see "The Great Commission" Matthew 28:16-20). Therefore, the more perfect our love becomes, the more we desire to pray for others, do charity, and spread the gospel of Jesus Christ. These things become a burden on your heart as they were a burden on Jesus's heart. God will make our hearts more like His.

Remember that love *grows* within you, and everyone grows in their own time. Only God loves perfectly, so it is important that we humble ourselves in knowing that we can never be perfect, but God can change our hearts, and He is the God that judges hearts.

When I texted my friend, "I forgive you," God was using me to show His love to someone else. God was also forcing me to believe in His truth about this person and what the young man could be with the love of Christ. The simple words "I forgive you" free a person from feelings of guilt that cause them to lose hope in the truth of God's love. Not only does forgiving a person free them, but it frees you. You no longer have to live in hurt, distrust, or bitterness toward anyone. On the contrary, you walk freely in knowing that God can produce the best characteristics in all of us. And by you being open to forgiving, God will show off the best fruit in you—LOVE.

Think About It

1. **Place your name in the blanks of 1 John 4:10.**

"Love is not that people love _____, but that _____ loves them and gives up _____'s life for _____'s brothers and sisters."

2. **List all the things you can do to show that you are giving up your life for your brothers and sisters.**

   a. _____

   b. _____

   c. _____

   d. _____

   e. _____

3. Are there any people that you have not forgiven? List them.

   a. _____

   b. _____

   c. _____

   d. _____

   e. _____

4. Read Ephesians 4:31-32 and explain what God says about forgiveness. How can you love the people you have not forgiven?

_____
_____
_____
_____

MY STORY – DERRICK

As a child, I loved my father with ease, He was always in and out of my life, but I loved my dad regardless of what he did.

But as I've grown older, I've started to define love based on my experiences, and I've started to put conditions on my love. My dad is really sick right now, and I don't care as much as I probably should. I feel bad for him on the basis that I would feel bad for any human being who was going through an illness, but I am not worried in the way someone should be for a father. If my mom just had the sniffles, I would be concerned. I just don't feel that way about my dad.

My disappointment in my father has put levels on my love, and my level of love for my father has diminished because of all the disappointments I've had with him. As a child, it was easy for me to love him, because I didn't really know what a father was supposed to be. I had no expectations. Most of my friends grew up without their fathers, so not having a dad wasn't strange to me. It was the norm. But once I got old enough to understand, I began to realize that I needed my dad, and he wasn't there. I wanted to give up my last name because I didn't even know the guy who gave it to me. I don't have sincere unconditional love for him. I've been thinking really logically about love. My logical human thinking tells me that I shouldn't be overwhelmed with worry about my dad's health when he was never all that worried about mine. But I'm Christian, and I know I shouldn't be thinking this way.

I know it's wrong. The way to fulfill what I should be doing in Christ is to not use what happened to me as an excuse for how I treat him. My dad was never really rooted in Christ. I didn't live with him, so I suppose he figured I was taken care of and as long as I was taken care of everything was fine. He thought of love on a logical level, and these days I am thinking that way too.

Nonetheless, I know my dad has love in him; he just has to unlock it. I know I'm supposed to show him love. The only difference Christians have from any other person is love. I have to share that with my dad. It's just been so difficult. Even so, it doesn't make sense for me to be in church and doing ministry but placing limitations on who gets my love. I'm basically limiting the work of ministry, and I'm limiting God.

So now I have chosen to pray. *Lord, help me, because I need the power of love to show the love that you have shown me. I need the gift of love to know how to love, how to truly forgive my dad, and how to get to a level of true ministry. Unlock unlimited forgiveness in me, because I haven't truly forgiven him. Help me to be humble and not arrogantly feel like I am better than my dad. Pull that love out me so I can pour it onto him.*

Chapter Four
The Gift of Love

Study Verse - *"Whatever is good and perfect comes down to us from God our Father, who created all the lights in the heavens. He never changes or casts a shifting shadow." James 1:17*

You're "a vessel, full of power, with a treasure from the Lord," sings Micah Stampley in *The Corinthian Song*[3]. The vessel is your flesh, the power is worked out in your soul, but the treasure is your spirit. If that spirit is filled with the Holy Spirit, you have an everlasting treasure filled with gifts and fruits of the Spirit that only our Father in heaven can provide. God gives the best gifts, and they are all free. But the greatest of all gifts is love.

In 1 Corinthians 13:1-3, Paul writes, "If I could speak all the languages of earth and of angels, but didn't love others, I would only be a noisy gong or a clanging cymbal. If I had the gift of prophecy, and if I understood all of God's secret plans and possessed all knowledge, and if I had such faith that could move mountains, but didn't love others, I would be nothing. If I gave everything I have to the poor and even sacrificed my body, I could boast about it, but if I didn't love others, I would have gained nothing."

God provides some amazing, perfect gifts, and Paul describes many of them here. But speaking in tongues, being able to prophesy about the future, having wisdom, knowledge, and faith to move mountains are mere baby cymbals compared to love. None of the other gifts even work correctly if they are not backed up by love. You may be able to sing in every key and memorize every scripture in the Bible, but if you do not have love, your works make a small ripple like a tiny stone thrown into the Atlantic Ocean. However, love gives a power akin to an earthquake with a seven-point Richter scale frequency, which will bring a ripple from the east coast of Japan to the west coast of the United States in a matter of hours.

Love is a gift provided to you by God through His Holy Spirit. In fact, love is a fruit of the Spirit. The characteristics of the fruit of the Spirit are literally within God's very nature. The fruits of the Spirit are love, joy, peace, patience, kindness, goodness, faithfulness, gentleness, and self-control. While non-Christians can act in love through their flesh (which we define in this book as "lust"), they will not have the eternal, Agape that God only provides as a fruit of His Holy Spirit. God's nature is to love, and therefore when you are filled with His Holy Spirit, love dwells within you.

Someone in their flesh cannot teach you how to love. Someone trying to get you to love them won't be able to if you have lost or never had the ability to love through the Holy Spirit.

Perfectly Loved: Knowing Love on God's Terms

Only God can change your heart and teach you how to love. You can fain the actions of love. But the creation of true eternal love is from God. Therefore, where there is a need for love, only God can get it to grow. You have the power to spread love through the Holy Spirit by planting and watering love to others. In the end, God will get the increase (growth).

I remember this fern my mom had in a small flowerpot in the back yard when I was growing up. It never died. My mom watered it every single day, and I remember it being there from the time I was probably six years old. Although it never died, it also never grew any bigger than the pot it was in. The plant was stagnant. When I was a teenager, I vividly remember my mom taking the fern out of the pot and planting it in the front yard. A few weeks later, I exclaimed to my mom about how big the fern had gotten. I never imagined it growing so big. My mom had watered the plant for so many years before, but it would not grow.

This is how God's fruit of love is. We can plant it and water it, but only God knows the conditions that it needs in order to get it to grow. God will get the increase. God will take it out of the tiny pot or box we may have put it in and give it the space it needs to grow.

You can pray for love to be implanted in you. You can pray for love to be implanted in others. You can even pray that the Holy Spirit provides you the wisdom and actions to be able to teach love to others. But at the end of the day, all love comes from God. It is a good and perfect gift, and it's available in infinities. Someone who asks for love will not be denied it, and someone who asks to share it will not be denied the ability to.

    I spent much of my post-adolescent life seeking love from men. Unfortunately, all the men I sought out were loveless. There was the boy bastardized by family and destroyed by childhood hurt that cursed love in all its ways. There was the boy with the vain perception of loving himself and no need to place love to others. And there was the boy so tarnished and displaced by love that he refused to even believe in it. It took going through the same situation three times for me to finally realize that I could not make anyone love me. Even after I gave my life to Christ, I placed myself into the same situation with the third boy. This time I did not acknowledge the fact that love comes from God and the most pure and perfect love cannot be taught by me but must be imprinted by the Lord. So while I attempted to teach love, I could not, as I had not given it unto the Holy Spirit to provide me the guidance to teach it, nor did I ever pray that the boy I was talking to would be able to receive it. So when he shut the door in my face, I found myself on my knees crying out, "Father, Father, why do I give love but I do not receive it in return? You said I should reap what I sow. But the reaping has not come." I could not reap what I was sowing, because what I was sowing had not been activated by the power of the Holy Spirit within me. I was attempting to make things happen through my fleshly thoughts and personal desires for gain.

Perfectly Loved: Knowing Love on God's Terms

How to Receive the Gift of Love

We are born of man in a sinful state and with a sinful nature because of the downfall of Adam and Eve. However, through the death of Jesus Christ we are made whole, and all that was once lost is now available to us through the Holy Spirit that lies within us once we believe. Within this, God provides and answers every prayer and will not withhold any gift from you as long as you ask in His name and pray to use it for His will. Love is available in infinities to everyone who believes in Him. He will not keep believers from receiving love, giving love, or being able to teach love. Because all of God's law is provided through love, he realizes that you cannot fulfill any of His promises or your Kingdom assignment without the gift of Love indwelling in your spirit naturally.

My ability to love does not come from me. At a young age, before I even knew what I was doing, I prayed for love to abound within me. That is one prayer that has continually been working within me from the day I requested it. In fact, I didn't just pray for His love; I wrote it as if I already had it. In hindsight, I realize I actually did. It's proven in my diary June 27, 2002, I was fourteen years old, and I wrote,

> "Sometimes I think I've been touched by an angel. I feel like He's in me. God's in me. I mean… I know a piece of Him is in everyone, but I think everyone has a different piece. But just like what piece of Him is in each person? I want His heart. I don't know if other people get a piece of His heart, but I'm sure that I want it."

Rhana A. Gittens

I don't know what God placed in me on that day to write that. I had never been to church other than a few Easter Sundays, and the Bible was foreign to me. All I knew of Jesus was His name. When I look back on that old diary, I am stunned by God and the realization that I was predestined to walk with love and share and teach love. On the very first day that I asked for His heart, He gave me a piece of His heart. (He already had it planned for me to ask.) Since then, and likely even before, the work of love has been working in me. At times I have felt stagnant and like no growth was there. But God was setting me up to change my conditions so that love could grow within me. I just had to obey Him when He pushed for condition changes and trust Him through the trials that would inevitably allow my love to grow. It was love that got me into a church, it was love that opened my ears to hear, it was love that got me saved and delivered, and it was love that the Holy Spirit now indwells in me. Thereby, the fruit of love continues to grow in me.

This explains even further how God's love is given. At the time I prayed for God's heart, I wasn't saved yet. I knew God, but I did not know Christ or the Holy Spirit. But the messenger of God said to Daniel in Daniel 10:12, "Don't be afraid. Since the first day you began to pray for understanding and to humble yourself before your God, your request has been heard in heaven. I have come in answer to your prayer." God gave me His heart on the first day I asked for it. He also destined me to one day come into salvation because He knew that I could not have His heart and love the way I wanted if I did not know Christ.

Perfectly Loved: Knowing Love on God's Terms

This gift was not just sent for me. It is for all of you. Pray for God's greatest gift, and it will be yours from the first day you ask. You may not feel an emotion after the prayer. You may not even see much change in surroundings and day-to-day life. However, be aware that after you pray for one of God's gifts, the Lord will change your conditions in order for that gift to grow in you so that the world can see the magnitude of its greatness. Like my mommy's fern, the next thing God will do is take you out of your special, perfectly placed pot and put you in the perfect place for your gifts to grow. Do not be afraid of the work God will do next.

Think About It

1. **Read 1 John 4:7-8 and personalize that scripture. First put your name in the blanks.**

1 John 4: 7-8 "Beloved, let us love one another, for love is of God; and everyone who loves is born of God and knows God. He who does not love does not know God, for God is love."

Let _____ love others, for love is of God; and when _____ loves _____ is born of God and knows God. When _____ does not love _____ does not love God, for God is love.

2. **Write about how this verse applies to you and how you can apply it your life.**

Rhana A. Gittens

_____
_____
_____
_____
_____
_____
_____
_____
_____

3. Do you know anyone who has an inability to receive love or an inability to give love? List those people. Feel free to acknowledge if you may be that person.

    a. _____

    b. _____

    c. _____

4. Read 1 John 4:7-8 and use it to say a prayer for love to abide in yourself and others. Write out your prayer here.

1 John 4: 7-8 "Beloved, let us love one another, for love is of God; and everyone who loves is born of God and knows God. He who does not love does not know God, for God is love."

_____
_____
_____
_____
_____

Perfectly Loved: Knowing Love on God's Terms

_____
_____
_____
_____

MY STORY- ALEX

The thought of quitting crosses my mind every day. There is always a second of doubt when I wonder if God is really with me. But there is something that keeps me motivated and takes away my fear.

In 2013, I quit my 9 to 5 to work my inspirational t-shirt business full-time. If you had talked to me five years ago, I would have told you I was going to be the founder of the most popular hip-hop brand. But God has told me different. If my purpose in life is to inspire people to find their own purpose and follow their dreams, then I have to be living that lifestyle. I had to live out what I was teaching. I had to let go of my own fears.

Unfortunately, before I ever got my business off the ground, I had created my own barriers that could have kept me from fulfilling my purpose. I thought money was a problem. I thought people wouldn't care. I thought I couldn't do it. I wanted to be a motivational speaker, but I felt like I didn't have adequate information to tell kids. I felt like I had to have some dramatic story. There were a lot of "I's."

Once I removed those barriers and started thinking, "Money isn't a barrier. People aren't a barrier. I can do it," everything opened up for me. When you start getting out of feelings of yourself and start recognizing that it's not about you, you are able to do it. For me, my problem was not that I was inadequate but that I was insecure. I let go of my insecurities and recognized that I didn't need anything special. I just needed something valuable to bring, whether I was a janitor or a man at a coffee shop. It was the devil making me feel like I didn't have the tools. He wanted me to feel powerless. But God's love gave me power, and his gifts made me empowered. God would never give me a feeling of inadequacy. God made me feel like I wouldn't fall climbing the mountain as long as I kept my eyes on Him.

My company is just in its infancy. I am building genuine relationships by talking to five people every day about something other than my business. From just talking to people, I see their fear, anxiety, and need for more of God. Because I know all the things people are worried about, I have been able to share those stories. I see the commonality in people and connect them through that. I am able to motivate them through their fears.

But because motivation is not just something I preach but a lifestyle I live, people are getting to know me. They either see that I am not who I use to be or that I am who I say I am. I'm not just selling my t-shirt business; I am uplifting people. More than that, what people are really doing is inspiring each other. When people buy the "Faith Over Fear" t-shirt, they walk around or share their pictures on social media, and all of a sudden eighty people have seen them with the shirt and eighty people have been inspired. My clothing company is preaching hope. People are becoming what they are wearing.

Nonetheless, I do sometimes doubt if God is still with me. I wonder if someone will actually come when I cry out for help. I realize that we are human and faith is a cute idea. However, we all definitely have actions that show we are underestimating God and doing things our own way. We don't always say, "I don't think God is with me," but we show it in our actions. I get over those doubts when I think of the blessings I can't see. When things go wrong, I am reminded that when God keeps me from one thing, He is saving me from something else.

Small moments remind me of God's presence. When someone mentions something I have done for them to someone else, and when people ask me for advice, it reminds me of my purpose. Those small moments of connection tell me that what I am doing is working. I say to people that the moment they state their dream out of their mouth, it is theirs. Of course they have to prove their weight, but that doesn't take the power away from them. You have to claim the victory that is already yours.

Thoughts of quitting run through my mind every day. Then I am reminded that I am a "hope dealer." My goal is to sell hopes and dreams to the people who need them. I am doing that through fashion. The only thing that could make me quit is if there was no love behind what I was doing. If there is no love and compassion behind it, then there is no fuel to continue. But my heart is rich right now. Not because I have million-dollar sales but because of the people who have been impacted. Love keeps me going.

Chapter Five
Love Expels Fear

Study Verse - *"There is no fear in love. But perfect love drives out fear, because fear has to do with punishment. The one who fears is not made perfect in love." 1 John 4:18 (NIV)*

First, I am assured of God's love because He sent Jesus to die for my sins.

Second, I am assured that God loves me because He lives within me.

Third, I can allow His love to do a work in me and be obedient to His call because I know love demolishes fear.

Fear is an emotion induced by a perceived threat that causes you to leave a location, hide, or not fulfill a task[4]. The operative word in this definition of fear is "perceived." Something or someone cannot induce fear in you unless you recognize, regard, or perceive it as a threat. Although there are threatening obstacles in our lives, the love God has for us protects us against the consequences of those obstacles, thereby, relieving our fears of them.

If you are flying on a plane, you identify that there is a possible threat of the plain crashing, but your recognition of God's love for you is greater than the perceived threat. Because you know God loves you and wouldn't do anything to harm you, you sit patiently in the plane in anticipation of its landing. Furthermore, you also recognize that even if the plane were to crash and if the crash were the cause of your death, God loves you and will protect you eternally and will continue to protect the loved ones you may leave behind. Even then, you sit on the plane in expectation of its safe landing. This is faith.

Faith demonstrates that when you know God loves you, your recognition of the perceived threat becomes minimal in comparison to your recognition of God's love for you. Your faith in God is greater than your fear.

We learn in God's Word and through experiences that God removes all threats and keeps us from harm when we are walking in His will. This does not mean that no bad will ever happen. On the contrary, it means that all things that do happen that are perceived as "bad" will inevitably work out for your good (Romans 8:28). Sometimes the best way to be reminded of God's love and faithfulness is to think about the past obstacles He has brought you through. When I was leaving college, I applied for a teaching job with Teach for America out of fear that I would not get a job after I graduated. But I didn't get the Teach for America job either. I was really upset about it. It made no sense to me that I would not get hired. But when it doesn't make sense, it's probably God. I realize that the fear I had of not getting a job was outweighing my faith in God. God blocked all of my plans and forced me to put full trust in Him. It would be more than a year after I graduated before I actually was hired in a position in my field. When my faith in His love became evident through my obedience, I saw Him rectifying my troubles and walking me into the beginnings of my dream career. If I had gotten the job with Teach for America or any of the other jobs I was rejected from, I would have gone into the wrong path for God's purpose for my life. I wouldn't be in the position I am now to author books, work in advertising, tutor other writers, and get a graduate degree. It all worked out for my good. He had a bigger plan. Remember God's faithfulness in the past. "If He did it before, He will do it again. Same God, right now. Same God, back then"[5].

Many Christians wrestle with understanding the full power of God's love and having full faith in it. I was challenged by it often. I would remind myself of God's promises, but later that fleshly, non-believing part of me would tell myself that those promises weren't really mine. In fact, in the midst of God telling me to write *Perfectly Loved*, I struggled with the fear of intimidation. However, God kept repeating to me, "Love expels fear."

In order to defeat fear, you must first recognize that you are fearful. Secondly, you need to determine what perceived threats are causing your fear. Thirdly, you must apply God's Word in proof and faith that His love covers them all. I have separated this study on fear so that we can tackle our fears of pursuing God's purpose for our life and our fears in relationships with others.

Expelling Our Fear of Pursuing God's Purpose

There are two types of fears that can take control of you when you are attempting to succeed, pursue a dream, or accomplish a divine goal that God has given you. The first is the fear of personal inadequacy and the second is the fear of an inadequate God. Let us expel both of those fear types today.

Fear Type 1: Fear that I am Inadequate

To feel inadequate is to experience a thought that you are lacking something to accomplish a need or meet a requirement. For example, suppose you are cooking blueberry pancakes for your girlfriend. You go through your pantry and pull out the oil, pancake mix, eggs, water, butter, and milk and then realize that you don't have the blueberries. You have everything you need to make regular pancakes, but you are discouraged because you didn't make the requirements to make the blueberry pancakes you promised your girlfriend. You are tempted to cancel breakfast plans altogether because there is no way you can make it to the store and back in time with the blueberries. You feel inadequate.

The fear of inadequacy is caused by the perceived threat of missing some ingredient such as time, support, money, education, friends, family, experience, location, position, timing, etc.

The Prophet Jeremiah had a fear of inadequacy. The Lord called Jeremiah and said, "I knew you before I formed you in your mother's womb. Before you were born I set you apart and appointed you as my prophet to the nations." But Jeremiah responded to God, "Hold it, Master God! Look at me. I don't know anything. I'm only a boy!" (Jeremiah 1: 5-6 MSG).

Imagine God Himself, the Great I Am in all His glory, walks into your church. There are 1,000 people in the chapel, but He comes in front of you and says, "I have chosen you out of your 1,000-member congregation to preach my Word from here to Asia to Africa to Europe the Americas and the Poles." And your only response is, "I'm sorry, God. No can do. I'm too young for that gig."

Guess what? God has chosen you out of the almost 7 billion people on the planet to do something special. And it's quite possible that you have responded, "No." You may not have uttered the word no, but your lack of action in accordance to God's specific plans illustrates the "no" in your heart.

Jeremiah had a perceived fear that his young age would keep people from listening to him. This fear was so great that He had the nerve, like many of us, to tell the Lord, the Great I Am, "No." Jeremiah's alleged lack of age and experience presented a fear of inadequacy and reluctance that was understandable from a human standpoint but not from God's standpoint.

The Prophet Jeremiah was around seventeen years old when God called him to ministry. He was ordained a prophet before birth (Jeremiah 1:5), and he was divinely empowered (Jeremiah 1:8-9) to predict destruction and restoration (Jeremiah 1:10)[6].

So are you. You were ordained for a purpose before you were born. Once you set your heart to believe in Christ's love, you were divinely empowered to fulfill your purpose. God did not ordain you at a point in time when you were qualified for the position. He called you before you were ever born. Once you set your heart, soul, and mind to say, "Yes, Lord, I'll do it," He equips you for the task. All you have to do is walk out on faith in His love.

The fear of inadequacy is based on "self" actions. It states that there is something "I" can't do. This fear is a fleshly, selfish fear that argues that the entire process of accomplishing the task is in some way based off of your own ingenious ability.

To get over the fear of inadequacy, you must get over yourself. Recognize that God gives you a choice of whether you want to follow Him or not. And after you make that choice, He alone endows you with the ability to accomplish the task He has given you.

Paul writes in Philippians 2:13, "For God is working in you, giving you the desire and the power to do what pleases Him." You must be humble and know that it is not by your own power that anything is going to be accomplished. You must release the chains of self-righteousness and embody God righteousness. But what happens when you don't believe in God's power either?

Fear Type II: Fearing that God is Inadequate

God responded to Jeremiah's reluctance by saying, "Don't say, 'I'm only a boy.' I'll tell you where to go and you'll go there.

I'll tell you what to say and you'll say it. Don't be afraid of a soul. I'll be right there, looking after you." God reached out and touched Jeremiah's mouth and said, "Look! I have just put my words in your mouth" (Jeremiah 1: 7-9).

God was trying to get Jeremiah to believe that not only was He giving him all the resources necessary to accomplish the task but that God was all powerful and would be there with him throughout the whole journey. He was not setting him up to start the journey, but He was equipping Jeremiah with everything he needed to complete it.

To illustrate a fear of an inadequate God, you are again making the blueberry pancakes for your girlfriend. This time you have the pancakes, eggs, butter, oil, water, and milk, and you remembered to get the blueberries. You laid out all the ingredients on the kitchen counter, but you just looked at them and never started cooking. On this occasion, you're not cooking because you don't think she will show up.

This is how we treat God sometimes. We know we have all the resources we need to accomplish the task, but we are afraid to do it alone. We don't think God will show up for His part. Have you ever felt like you had been starting something in obedience to God, but He wasn't there?

"Yes, God, you gave me the building, the money, the inspiration to start my own restaurant, but you said you would take care of getting the restaurant patrons. I'm open for business, and no one is here. I'm afraid you walked out on me on your end of the bargain. Where are you now, God? I thought you were in this with me."

Those feelings are painful, but we have to constantly remind ourselves that God has not left us. This is all a part of the plan. God is testing how far your faith in His love will go. If He told you to start a restaurant and it completely crashed and burned, would you still trust Him? God gives us instructions in order to build our character. Having faith in God's love is also having faith that though you may not see the success you sought after, the good God was seeking through your obedience was accomplished, and in that you have the victory.

When you fear that God is inadequate, you believe that there is some type of lack in Him. You may believe that He isn't working fast enough or He just doesn't love you enough. Trust that God sees more than what we could ever imagine. His timing is not our timing. A year for us is but a second to Him. If He told you to start a restaurant, and you don't break even until five years later, He is still God. Some people will not make it through to year five because they will lose faith in His power. But others will be reminded of the promise of love that God gave them and wait for His timing. Who will you be? Will you ditch the mission or stay on until God shows His face?

The Bible has numerous stories illustrating the great faith of our ancestors. Noah stayed on the arc with his wife, sons, and stinky animals for an entire year before the water subsided and He could get on dry land. (Genesis 7:17-8:22). The sick woman forced herself beneath the legs of the crowd surrounding Jesus just to touch the hem of His robes to be healed after thirteen years with a blood disorder (Mark 5:25-34). These are examples of faith in God's powerful love to do what He said He would do. These stories of faith do not end with the Bible. They continue through you.

On the other side of faith is recognizing that you cannot accomplish your purpose without God. You can have all the resources in the world and you may even be successful for a while, but the success God seeks for us is not of this world but eternal. Can you get eternal victory without God?

When you recognize that your gifts are nothing without God backing them up, you release yourself onto Him and allow Him to use you as He chooses. God cannot use you when you are self-righteous and convinced that you control your own destiny. When you are thinking on your own abilities, you tend to shift the plan and make it your own. When you are moving on God's grace and power, you move with Him and not before Him, always toward Him and not away from Him.

From the first time you called on God to clean your heart, He came and began giving you new desires that were in line with your Kingdom-driven purpose and assignment. Not only did He give you the desire to pursue that dream, but He graced you with the ability, resources, and power to achieve it. By Jesus's death, you were graced with the forgiveness of your sins along with the power to do anything under the sun in God's name with the power of the Holy Spirit. You are right to believe you are completely undeserving of this grace. You didn't have to do anything to receive it except to believe that Jesus Christ died for your sins and rose again. God set grace up in this fashion to humble us by the magnificent thought of life-changing love. Within your humbleness, you need to take action with the righteous power and gifts that God has placed over you through His Spirit.

Applying the Word of God to your fears is the best way to expel them. Every time you think of a perceived fear, pray the Word of God over it and acknowledge His power to protect you from it. As you live this out daily, it will dwell in your Spirit forever, and you will be able to walk through God's call on your life.

Pray About It - *"I will acknowledge that my perceived fear of being incapable of attaining the purpose God has placed in my life is an illegitimate fear. He is not only giving me the desire to fulfill the purpose but also giving me the power and ability to attain it through Him. I pray that God's love will expel my fears of my own inability. I pray that God will change my heart to understanding that He will grace me and provide me with all I need to fulfill the purpose He has for my life."*

Love Expels Our Fears in Relationships with Others

The title of this chapter is "*Love* Expels *Fear.*" In this section, *Love* is *you* with the power of Christ. The *Fear* we are combating is other people's perception of *you* and God as a threat. People have an illegitimate fear of *you* and of God. Again, they see you and God as a threat.

However, when you operate in God's love, you cause others to be able to trust you, confide in you, create healthy relationships with you, feel protected and safe with you, and not fear loving you back. Your love for them expels their fears of the fleshly, selfish things that unloving people do. In addition, when you operate in godly love you make people less afraid of God. He uses you to shower His love on others and expel their fears.

There is only one over-arching fear type when it comes to fear in relationships with God and others. It is simply the fear of getting hurt. The fear of getting hurt is characterized by the numbered threats listed below. Under each thought is a verse that combats that fear and an explanation on how you can apply the verse when you feel this perceived threat coming up in yourself.

1. I am afraid that people will judge me incorrectly and I will be misunderstood.

"For the Lord is our judge, our law giver, and our king. He will care for us and save us." Isaiah 33:22

God runs this thing. People who are not living in God's love may judge us, and even those people who mean the best may misunderstand us. Only God truly can judge our hearts and characters. Because He runs this thing, do not be afraid that anyone's judgment against you can make or break you. God has the final judgment.

2. I am afraid of being seen for who I really am because who I really am isn't so good.

"So the Lord sent Nathan the prophet to tell David the story... Then David confessed to Nathan. 'I have sinned against the Lord.'" 2 Samuel 12:1, 13

God calls us to be vulnerable and accountable to others within the body of Christ. We are not expected to be perfect, but we are expected to help perfect each other. By releasing your fear of being vulnerable and showing others your weakness, you allow God to shape your character and expel your weaknesses.

3. I am afraid of setting expectations for someone and them not delivering.

"The lame man looked at them eagerly, expecting some money. But Peter said, 'I don't have any silver or gold for you. But I'll give you what I have. By the name of Jesus Christ the Nazarene, get up and walk!" Acts 3:4

Sometimes we set an expectation for someone to give something to us or help us with something specific. They may not fulfill the initial expectation because they can't or they just won't. However, God will fulfill this expectation. The important lesson to learn is not to put your expectation in the person but to put your expectation in God. Your needs are fulfilled through Him, and He may put people in your presence to handle those tasks, but all expectancy should be on God alone.

4. I am afraid of being forgotten by someone or being left out.

"Can a mother forget her nursing child? Can she feel no love for the child she has borne? But even if that were possible, I would not forget you! See, I have written your name on the palms of my hands." Isaiah 49:15-16

God promises that we are never forgotten. When people forget us and when family forsakes us, we must hold on to the promise that God has not forgotten us. His remembrance of us is truly all we need. Remind yourself of this equation—Me plus God is Everything. Me minus everyone else plus God is still Everything. When you find yourself alone, God draws closer to you; the power of His love is greater than that of people.

5. I am afraid of my love for someone not being reciprocated.

"They went out from us, but they were not of us; for if they had been of us, they would have continued with us; but they went out that they might be made manifest, that none of them were of us." 1 John 2:19 (KJV)

True love has a permanent quality. If a person truly loves you, they will always be there. You have to question what you define as "being there." Some people are only meant to be acquaintances, others close friends, others romantic partners, some family, and some teachers. When you fear unrequited or unreciprocated love, find out what type of "love" relationship it is you are looking for. If someone loves you with Agape love, the form of the relationship is not what we are to fear. Agape love is a permanent quality more than a state of being. It could be possible that you are looking for a romantic relationship where they are just looking for friendship. If this is so, then you do not fear them not loving you, but you fear not having the relationship with them that you prefer. So your fear may be more about your state of love than theirs.

However, if someone does not have the love of God within them, they may leave you. Keep in mind that in this case, there was no good in having them with you anyway, because they were not meant to continue the journey with you. Their part in your story may be over.

6. I am afraid that this person will try to change me.

"So all of us who have had that veil removed can see and reflect the glory of the Lord. And the Lord—who is the Spirit—makes us more and more like him as we are changed into his glorious image." 2 Corinthians 3:18

When God's Spirit dwells in us, He sets out to accomplish a change within us. He wants us to be transformed to be more like Him. Within this process, you may meet people who will try to keep you accountable toward that renewal and push you along in your transformation to being more like Christ. However, your task will be to determine what people were sent from God to help you grow in Him and what people are not from Him. There will be people who are acting outside of God's will. Praying for discernment and wisdom will help you distinguish these people. In addition, knowing God's Word will help you determine if the advice you are getting will bring you closer to God or have the effect of pulling you away from Him.

7. I am afraid that this person is not trustworthy and that I cannot confide in them.

"For the word of God is alive and powerful. It is sharper than the sharpest two-edged sword, cutting between soul and spirit, between joint and marrow. It exposes our innermost thoughts and desires. Nothing in all creation is hidden from God." Hebrews 4:12

One gift that comes with God's love is the gift of discernment. You may not always walk in the full gift, but you will have moments of wisdom about people. You will receive wisdom from others about a person, receive revelation from the Word of God, or God will show you who that person really is through their actions. No matter which way the discerning wisdom comes, it is your choice to follow it. "When someone shows you who they are, believe them the first time," (Maya Angelou).

8. I am afraid of being jealous of this person or them being jealous of me.

"There are different kinds of spiritual gifts, but the same Spirit is the source of them all. There are different kinds of service, but we serve the same Lord. God works in different ways, but it is the same God who does the work in all of us." 1 Corinthians 12:4-6

God's perfect love is so perfect that He bestows that exact same love to each and every one of us. None of us get more or less. We are all receiving 100 percent of the same package of love. The gifts and blessings God bestows on us are all equally important. We are one body. The foot may not get as much attention as the brain, but the person with a mind to run a mile cannot do it without the foot. Though jealousy may show its crooked little face, your knowledge of the truth will help you suppress thoughts of jealousy inside of your heart and react with God's love when other people's acts of jealousy come against you.

9. I am afraid of being used by others for their own selfish gain.

"What good is it, dear brothers and sisters, if you say you have faith but don't show it by your actions? Can that kind of faith save anyone? Suppose you see a brother or sister who has no food or clothing, and you say, 'Good-bye and have a good day; stay warm and eat well' – but then you don't give that person any food or clothing. What good does that do?" James 2: 14-16

Use me up! God requires you to give no matter the circumstances. If you see a homeless panhandler asking for money, you have no idea what they may do with that money. But it is not your job to manage what that person does. It is your job to manage your heart for giving. I once heard a statement that 90 percent of panhandlers are just looking for drug money. Well, I say give anyway, because you never know when you have met someone from the 10 percent who truly need it. If the person does something illegitimate with the money, God will reap the consequences on them. If you do not give out of obedience to Him, God will reap the consequences on you. When necessary, God will grace you with wisdom and tell you when He does not want you to give or help. Either way, it is your job to obey and not your job to manage what happens with your giving. Give unto God at all times, and He will manage the increase.

10. I am afraid of hurting someone else.

We have learned from acknowledging our fears of getting hurt and applying God's Word against them that God teaches us how to treat people. He insures that His love is presented beautifully within us so that we can go out and love others the way He loves us. Nevertheless, we will make mistakes, unintentional and intentional. When we acknowledge an error, we pray and request reconciliation and forgiveness from others. Never hurting anyone does not make you a loving person. Apologizing and handling your mistakes the way God requires makes you a loving person.

God's love helps us to expel our fear of walking out on God's purpose and our fear of people. It also expels people's fear of us and God. The Holy Spirit does not want us to be afraid of people because we have been given a Spirit of power, love, and self-discipline that would allow us to be wise and enjoy being with people (2 Timothy 1:7). We are called to be courageous, take the initiative, and walk in loving fellowship with others, not fear.

We must acknowledge our fears in order to remove them. Do not be afraid to read through all of the fear characteristics we made in this chapter and acknowledge to yourself that you might have some of these fears. More than anything, remember that God is not the producer of fear but the expeller of these perceived threats.

In Mark 3:3-5 is the story of Jesus's healing of a man on the Sabbath. On the Sabbath, Jesus said to the man with the deformed hand, "'Come and stand in front of everyone. ... Hold out your hand.' So the man held out his hand, and it was restored." Do you think being a minority, a woman, young, or inexperienced is holding you back from doing God's work? Like the man with shriveled hand, God wants to use you to show His glory, power, and might. Someone might be telling you that you're unqualified, but God is here to qualify you to do His Will. Make Him proud to use you and have you "stand up in front of everyone" to show the great works He has done in and through you.

You truly are the best thing that God ever made. You are the only one who can accomplish what God called you to do. You are the only one with the set of experiences and network of connections that will allow God to accomplish the task He set forth when you were created. You were nowhere near a mistake or luck of chance when you were born. You were meant to be here. Your life affects so many people around you. You are a precious gift to the world. Don't be afraid to go out and do what God created you for.

Rhana A. Gittens

Think About It

1. What is a goal, purpose, or dream God has lain on your heart?

   _____
   _____
   _____

2. What fears could hinder you from achieving your goals?

   _____
   _____
   _____

3. Find a Bible verse that expunges/negates that fear.

   _____
   _____
   _____

4. Pray for God's love to expel your fear.

   _____
   _____
   _____

Perfectly Loved: Knowing Love on God's Terms

MY STORY- COURTNEY

For me the adversity began when I was born and it just continued from there. I grew up without a dad in my life and it was a serious struggle for me. I remember being eight years old and getting dressed up waiting for him to pick me up. I sat at that window all day and he never came. I always asked God, "Why did you curse me with a horrible father who hurt me before anyone else could?" I never believed that pain would go away. I prayed that God would make my dad want me.

There was a scene in the movie *Drumline* starring Nick Cannon. He was contemplating inviting his dad to graduation. He went to his dad's job and threw a graduation ticket at him. He said, "I've been coming down here every day for the last two weeks thinking if I should give you that ticket to my graduation. Now I changed my mind. Look, man. I just want to let you know that I got my diploma. I ain't never been arrested. I don't have a whole bunch of kids running around. Unlike yourself, I'm doing something with my music. I got a full scholarship to Atlanta A & T playing the drums. I want to say, I hope you're proud 'cause I made it without you"[7]. I dreamed of the day I would be able to play out that scene with my own father.

I was troubled and misunderstood. I had to cook, clean, and watch my younger siblings when my mom was at work. I got into a lot of fights. I was still an 'A' student, but my attitude was so bad that my mom got really upset and said, "You're going to turn out like your dad." The one thing I knew was that I didn't want to turn out like him. I believe God loved me so much that He brought someone in my life to keep me from turning into something undesirable. My high school mentor loved me in a way that I never had a man love me. He was the first person I met who had graduated from college. He gave me a reason to want to be better. Now I have two degrees. While my dad wasn't in the picture, God brought love in my life through someone else in order to help me through those struggles.

But I still had parts of me that needed to be worked on. I've always been bad at picking and choosing my battles wisely. I have always been very defensive. There came a point where God had to teach me some lessons the hard way. In doing that, I got shot. Before the guy shot me, all I was thinking was, "I need to beat this man's a**." But after that bullet hit me, my life took a turning point. That was the pinnacle moment of my life that I realized if I didn't stop thinking I had to defend myself against the world, I would die. God's love is strong enough to fight my battles, but I had to let Him.

The characteristic of God that has helped me most in my life has been His unconditional love. I was given some hard cards to play at times in life and in many moments I handled those situations poorly. But God continued to love me unconditionally. He spared my life because, to Him, I am someone worth sparing. That is enough for me to continue moving forward and walking in His will.

Adversity is like a tunnel. It's dark, and you can't see the exit. You don't want to go through the darkness, but somehow you have to know that there is a light down there at the end. I get through because I know my God is going to get me through it, and He is shining a light for me to follow at the end of that tunnel.

As long as I trust that God has my back and I am doing all I can to please him, I know I'll get through it. Hard times have caused me to be humble when victory comes knocking at my door. Now I can share my story with others who have gone through similar situations. It isn't easy, but I make sure to always remember God's love while I'm going through it.

Rhana A. Gittens

Chapter Six
Love Through Adversity

Study Verse - *"Faith is the confidence that what we hope for will actually happen; it gives us assurance about things we cannot see." Hebrews 11:1*

With everything that is going on in the world today, it gets harder and harder to have faith in love. Some of the most difficult conversations about God that I have had have been with people who were homeless and sick. One of my close friends once said to me, "God doesn't love me." I asked why he thought that. He responded, "I can't get a job. I'm basically homeless. I haven't eaten in a week, and God hates me."

I listened to him, and I understood his pain. But I didn't agree with his conclusion.

I am reminded of the scenes on the news after the 7.0 earthquake in Haiti. The *New York Times* reported:

"Five days after Haiti's devastating earthquake, an evangelical pastor in a frayed polo shirt, his church crushed

Perfectly Loved: Knowing Love on God's Terms

but his spirit vibrant, sounded a siren to summon the newly homeless residents of a tent city to an urgent Sunday prayer service.

Voice scratchy, eyes bloodshot, arms raised to the sky, the Rev. Joseph Lejeune urged the hungry, injured and grieving Haitians who gathered round to close their eyes and elevate their beings up and out of the fetid Champ de Mars square where they now scrambled to survive. 'Think of our new village here as the home of Jesus Christ, not the scene of a disaster,' he called out over a loudspeaker. 'Life is not a disaster. Life is joy! You don't have food? Nourish yourself with the Lord. You don't have water? Drink in the spirit.'

And drink they did, singing, swaying, chanting and holding their noses to block out the acrid stench of the bodies in a collapsed school nearby. Military helicopters buzzed overhead, and the faithful reached toward them and beyond, escaping for a couple of hours from the grim patch of concrete where they sought shelter under sheets slung over poles.

In varying versions, this scene repeated itself throughout the Haitian capital on Sunday. With many of their churches flattened and their priests and pastors killed, Haitians desperate for aid and comfort beseeched God to ease their grief. Carrying Bibles, they traversed the dusty, rubble-filled streets searching for solace at scattered prayer gatherings.⁸"

For those with no belief in God, those with shallow faith, and the most mature Christians, this was a stunning sight. No matter where you were in your walk with God, everyone learned a new level of faith by watching the Haitians praise and worship after the devastation that hit their country. It was astonishing, because no one would blame them if they did not praise God. Everyone would understand that it's hard to praise God in the midst of such fierce adversity.

However, it is not so insane of a reaction when you think about Christianity itself. Our religion was birthed out of the torture, crucifixion, and death of our Savior Jesus Christ. It was born out of adversity. Knowing this, the scene of the Haitians' praise is no longer insane at all. Though Christianity was born out of adversity, Jesus rose. His rising signifies to all believers that though we go through turmoil in this life, there is an eternal rising in the afterlife that will make all the trials and sacrifices worth it. For the Haitians, their suffering had eternal meaning. God would help them endure and make it through to see another blessed day on earth. Even if God decided to end it all today, they would still see a blessed day with Him in heaven. They trusted in God's love and the eternal blessing that was promised to them in the midst of all trials. They remembered this spiritual vision rather than renouncing their faith.

The Haitians put faith in action. Hebrews 11:1 says, "Faith is the confidence that what we hope for will actually happen; it gives us assurance about things we cannot see". It's a blessing to see people still praising God despite what they are going through. We have to be grateful for these people, because they remind us of God's faithfulness. They remind us of God's love. They remind us that through His love we can all endure adversity.

Adversity is any affliction, calamity, or stress. It may cause you sorrow and torment. The first thing to remember about adversity is that it doesn't only come from the devil. The devil can do nothing without God allowing it. Enemies are often God's instruments to impose discipline on His people. Remember, these are divine chastisements, and God knows exactly what you can tolerate. Trials and tribulations come from God for multiple reasons.

The authors of Hebrews 12:5-9 write that God said, "My child, don't make light of the Lord's discipline, and don't give up when he corrects you. For the Lord disciplines those He loves, and He punishes each one He accepts as His child. As you endure this divine discipline, remember that God is treating you as His own children. Who ever heard of a child who is never disciplined by its father? If God doesn't discipline you as He does all of His children, it means that you are illegitimate and are not really His children at all."

In the New King James Version, it is written like this: "My son do not despise the chastening of the Lord." Chastening is more correctly translated from the Greek as training or education[9]. When we receive discipline from our earthly parents, we do not view this as a sign that they hate us. As we grow older, we realize that they were attempting to educate us, and it was actually a sign of their love. Similarly, when God allows suffering, it is not an indication that He dislikes us, nor is it always a signal that we have done something wrong and need to be punished. God utilizes adversity to cultivate our characters and remove anything not like Him from within us. His discipline molds us into His image. The trials you go through today may possibly be setting you up for victory in the future so that you know how to handle the issues that are to come. His discipline trains us for the real battles and strengthens us to be victorious in our walk with Him. Even natural disasters somehow become a place for God's love to be shown through the selflessness of people who respond to crisis. In addition, these disasters, when they destroy entire cities, give a chance for a new birth of that city and renewal of its people.

Secondly, the NKJV version of Hebrews 12:6 says don't be discouraged when you are "rebuked by Him." To rebuke is to convict or convince[10]. The term "rebuke" is often understood with a negative connotation. However, rebuking implicitly blesses us, as God uses adversity to convince His people of the truth thereby causing their wrong actions to change. For some people, God can be subtle in order to convince them that they need to change. But with others, He may have to go all out. Regardless, He wants us to be better, so He puts us through different levels of fire in order to correct us.

We all know our children. We have some children that you only have to tell once to clean their room and they do it. But you may have a more stubborn child that you have to let live in their own filth before they realize the importance of cleaning their room.

Regardless of how the education may come, God will teach us. He loves us too much to let us sink in our sin.

Lastly, the NKJV version says that God "scourges every son who He receives." To scourge is to flog or whip either literally or figuratively[11]. This signifies that God also uses adversity to punish. This was especially prevalent in the Old Testament. When the Israelites turned their back on God, He would send destruction to their towns (Hebrews 3:8-11). Divine punishment is a blessing. It not only convinces us of our wrongdoing, but it leads us back to fellowship with our Father in heaven. Punishment brings us to a level of brokenness where you must turn to God to bring you out. When you turn your back on God and forget Him, He may bring suffering in your life so that you have no choice but to run to Him for help out of it. He is reminding you who He is.

Enemies may be instruments to inflict our adversity, but these trials are still divine chastisements. God has his hand in it all. It is great to know that God knows the struggle you are feeling and will always make a way for you to escape. In Hebrews 12:11, the authors remind us of one of God's promises. "No discipline is enjoyable while it is happening—it's painful! But afterward there will be a peaceful harvest of right living for those who are trained in this way." There is a promise for a harvest. Faith in God's love is put to the test when we are faced with adversity. In order to put faith in action, you must know God's promises in the midst of adversity. We will go through each of God's promises one by one and then discover faith in action.

Rhana A. Gittens

PROMISE ONE: God Avenges

David is an everlasting example of someone who truly believed that God would fight all of His battles. After King Saul finally died, Saul still had another son, Ishbosheth, who could possibly retrieve the throne before David. Two of David's followers, Recab and Baanah, took it into their own hands to kill Ishbosheth. When David found out, he said to them, "The Lord, who saves me from all my enemies, is my witness. Someone once told me, 'Saul is dead,' thinking he was bringing me good news. But I seized him and killed him at Ziklag. That's the reward I gave him for his news. How much more should I reward evil men who have killed an innocent man in his own house and on his own bed?" (2 Samuel 4:9-11). Saul specifically says to Recab and Baanah that God saves him from his enemies. He did not need them to avenge him.

When I think of Recab and Baanah, I see the Marvel comic super heroes "The Avengers." Recab and Baanah swooped in like Iron Man, the Hulk, Thor, and Captain America and thought they were saving the day for David to get Saul's throne. David had them killed for putting vengeance in their own hands rather than leaving the future up to God (2 Samuel 4). God had already promised the kingdom to David. David had faith that God would work it all out to fulfill the promise.

God always avenges us. Saul hunted David for approximately four years. David had chances where he could have killed Saul, but he never did. He knew that the battle was God's.

Perfectly Loved: Knowing Love on God's Terms

David's faith in God's vengeance proved correct. Saul inevitably committed suicide when he thought the Philistines were going to kill him in battle (1 Samuel 31). David never had to get his hands dirty. God embodies the four Avengers in one. He has all of their powers and more.

In Psalm 10:13, David asked, "Why do the wicked get away with despising God?" Then he answers his own question when he realizes that the wicked are not getting away with anything. God takes note of all they do and defends His people.

In the midst of persecution from our enemies, we must always remember that God defends us. He sees and He hears what we are going through. Because David went through so much adversity from people, reading Psalms when we are in the midst of our own trials is a great way to be encouraged. Though things seem bleak for us at the time, David's psalms poetically remind us that "You (God) see the trouble and grief they cause. You take note of it and punish them. The helpless put their trust in you. You defend the orphans." (Psalm 10:14)

It is important to note that David specifically states that God will defend "orphans." By orphans, he is referring to all that are alone and have no defense. God draws closest to those who are weakest and have no other protection. He fights for you because He refuses to lose you. You have a shining light inside of you, and He doesn't want it be dimmed. Rather, He wants your light to shine bright throughout your struggles so that others can see it in the midst of the darkness.

Rhana A. Gittens

PROMISE TWO: God provides love through others to see us through adversity.

He provides His protection through the love and kindness we receive from others. Friends, family, and neighbors allow us to experience God's love. God didn't promise that there wouldn't be trouble. But He promised that His love would see us through to the end so that we would be victorious.

Simon, a disciple of Jesus, had a sick mother-in-law in bed with the fever. Simon told Jesus about his sick loved one, and Jesus came to her bedside took her by the hand and helped her sit up. Her fever went away (Mark 1: 29-31). Although Jesus was the one doing the healing, Simon was the one who brought Jesus to her.

Our family and friends bring Jesus to us when they give us a ride home after our car breaks down, help us when we are moving, celebrate our birthdays and successes, listen to our fears, or tend to us when we are sick. All of these moments are God's love moments.

Those moments feel so good too. When I moved to Atlanta, I basically knew no one and had no close friends or relatives nearby. However, God showed me His love in that overwhelmingly lonely circumstance. Around the corner of every trial I faced was always some person helping me through it. When I had no place to stay for an interview trip, God connected me to a friendly home through my best friend. When I needed help finding an apartment, my friends nearly trampled me with love, suggestions, and action. People were willing to help me pack, move, and find a roommate with no questions and no money needed. When I sat in my new apartment all alone, God brought me a church family and a friendly neighbor. Just simple issues like needing a ride to the airport or someone to help me carry my heavy new dining room table up three flights of stairs were all handled by strangers. In all these instances and more, I felt God's love for me. I hadn't done anything special for any of these people, yet they were showing me so much kindness. I knew that it was my Lord and Savior using them to remind me that He was with me on the new journey in my life.

PROMISE THREE: Adversity prepares you for future victory

God said to Jeremiah, "If racing against mere men makes you tired, how will you race against horses?" (Jeremiah 12:5). If you fail under the pressures of adversity that God puts before you, then your strength needs strengthening. You cannot expect to be victorious throughout your life's journey if you do not allow God to prepare you for it. God puts roadblocks in the way today to get you ready for all that you will go through tomorrow in order to fulfill your purpose. The things that you stress over now may not even cause you to wince when you come against them later on.

When I think of adversity as preparation for future victory, I think of Joseph (Genesis 37-50). Joseph was the son of Jacob, and at a young age he had a dream that he would one day rule over his brothers. However, before he ever got to that point, his brothers sold him into slavery. Thankfully, he was purchased by Potiphar, an Egyptian officer and captain of the guard for Pharaoh. Joseph was so good at the work he did that Potiphar made Joseph his personal assistant. Unfortunately, Potiphar's wife lied about Joseph

Rhana A. Gittens

to Potiphar, stating that Joseph tried to sleep with her. Joseph was thrown into prison. In prison, he interpreted the dreams of Pharaoh's chief cupbearer and chief baker. Pharaoh eventually released the chief cupbearer from prison, and two-years after his release, Pharaoh had a dream and needed it interpreted. The chief cupbearer remembered Joseph. When Joseph was summoned and able to interpret Pharaoh's dream, Pharaoh placed Joseph in charge of Egypt. When the famine came, Joseph's brothers traveled from Canine to Egypt. They did not know that the man they would be asking for food would be the same man they sold into prison. Joseph went through trial after trial, but all of it led to his inevitable position as second in command over Egypt.

Your adversity is also leading you on a path. Depending on how your faith works within those trials, you could be able to see victory at the end. But if you do not obey God, and if you try to get out of the trial too early, or if you try to put matters in your own hands, you may not see the success God had for you in the end.

Our study scripture for this chapter is Hebrews 11:1: "Faith is the confidence that what we hope for will actually happen; it gives us assurance about things we cannot see."

In the beginning of this chapter, I mentioned a transient friend of mine with no home to call his own. Despite his bachelor's degree, he had difficulty finding steady employment, and he had nearly given up on expecting help from any one because he felt that everyone he knew had all let him down. I often wonder how to give advice to people in such turmoil. I consistently urged him to have faith. I asked him to forgive those who had hurt him and to

Perfectly Loved: Knowing Love on God's Terms

forgive himself for the wrongs he had done. But because his eyes were closed to the love of Jesus Christ, nothing I said ever got through. It was like talking to a moving ocean wave. You may tell the waves to stop, but no matter what you do, they just keep crashing. His lack of faith in God caused him to just keep crashing. All I could do was plant the seeds of faith and pray that God would water them and establish the increase.

For my friend, faith in and of itself made no common sense. In fact, faith makes no common sense to common man. Faith forces you to believe in something you can't hear, feel, or smell. But "just because you can't see the air doesn't keep you from breathing. And just because you can't see God doesn't keep you from believing," said the six-year-old character Jeremiah Biggs in the 1996 film *The Preacher's Wife*[12]. You have to have faith just to believe in creation of the universe. God and His Word were the only ones present for the creation, so you have to take His word for it. The world says, "Seeing is believing" but God says, "believing is seeing," writes William MacDonald[13].

However, you can't just have faith in anything. You have to have faith in some promise, revelation, or conviction from God. God's promises are the foundation of faith. The biggest faith is when you believe in something that is impossible with the knowledge that with God it is possible. Adversity is just a way to test faith in order to see if it is real to you. Without faith, you can't have love, and without love it is impossible to please God. Love is faith in action.

Rhana A. Gittens

Therefore, when we are faced with the myriad of trials that come to us from all directions, what is it that keeps us from giving up? There are people who commit suicide because the adversity hurts so much, but there are others who refuse to surrender. What is the common denominator among those who refuse to give up despite their hardships? I argue that faith in something causes people to keep going. Nonbelievers may have so much faith in their own selves or money or family that they would never give up. When they become weak, money passes away, or family walks out, what do those people have? Believers have faith in a constant force that is unmovable and unshakeable. Believers have a sustaining vigor that allows their faith to not only be there but also grow at an accelerating pace. Through adversity and trials, God gives us reasons to increase our faith. He presses, molds, shapes, and strengthens our resolve for Him. It keeps us from having any reason to question His abilities.

Love is just faith in action. So when we have faith that God will repay our love with more love, we act more lovely. Again, we have faith in His promises. Therefore, in order to fully encompass faith within yourselves, you must know God's promises, which comes from reading His Word. He watches after His Word to perform it (Jeremiah 1:12).

I leave you with one last promise:

In Romans 8:35-39 Paul writes, "Can anything ever separate us from Christ's love? Does it mean He no longer loves us if we have trouble or calamity, or are persecuted, or hungry, or destitute, or in danger, or threatened with death? No, despite all these things, overwhelming victory is ours through Christ, who loved us. And I am convinced that nothing can ever separate us from God's love. Neither death, nor life, neither angels nor demons, neither our fears for today nor our worries about tomorrow—not even the powers of hell can separate us from God's love. No power in the sky above or in the earth below—indeed, nothing in all creation will ever be able to separate us from the love of God that is revealed in Christ Jesus our Lord."

Think About It

1. **Describe a current obstacle you are facing.**

   _____

   _____

   _____

   _____

2. **What do you think is the reason for this obstacle? (Circle one or more)**

   Chastening: Discipline, Training, and Education

   Rebuking: Conviction and Convincing

   Scourge: Punishment

3. **What led you to choose this reasoning?**

   _____

   _____

Rhana A. Gittens

4. What is God's promise through this adversity?

5. What is the promise in Romans 8:35-39?

6. How would you encourage someone else going through the same obstacle?

Perfectly Loved: Knowing Love on God's Terms

MY STORY - AMAZ

"Penny." That's what he called me.

I thought he was talking about Penny Proud from Disney Channel's "The Proud Family", because you know, "I'm cute and I'm loud and I got it going on."

But that wasn't it at all. He was calling me "Penny" because of my skin color. I reminded him of a penny. Now I embrace my mocha copper skin color. I'm proud of it, but there was a time when I wasn't.

I have a tattoo that reads "Black is Beauty," because I was teased about my complexion growing up. A guy once told me I would be really pretty if I was light skinned. As a kid, a teen, and even into parts of college, I questioned everything about myself. *Why do I look this way? Why am I so emotional? Why am I so open to people?* I wondered why God made me this way. Why did God give me such a big heart? I felt like my openness just set people up to hurt me.

I started to realize that everything I am is for my calling. Nothing was by mistake. He knew what I would need. He knew the doors that certain attributes of my personality would open. Over time, I have learned to embrace my personality. I am starting to believe that I am fearfully and wonderfully made. It's not just a cliché. I believe that who I am and all that I have is for a reason.

Despite the progress I have made toward loving myself, accepting all of who I am wasn't a conscious decision. Sometimes it was a situation or a person who spoke to me. Like the guy who

Rhana A. Gittens

called me "Penny." He meant it as a compliment. He said my skin tone was unique. Having someone else—a random stranger at the time—point out what I deemed to be my biggest setback helped me to embrace who I am. I became in love with me.

When I was writing my graduate school essay, I realized that I have always been who I am today. I just perfected certain things. As a child, I was very talkative and starting a conversation with a stranger was a daily occurrence. Not much has changed. Being loquacious has made me very successful in business, especially my career in sales. At the end of the day, I can only be who God created me to be. There is a calling that God has placed on my life, and He made me with the exact skill sets that I have, because He knew I needed them to fulfill the purpose He had for my life.

There was a time when I forgot about God's promises. I felt that if I disappointed God enough, He wouldn't be proud of me. I began to humanize God and bring him down to my level. If a person didn't return my phone call in a certain period of time, I thought they didn't care. That's how I felt about God.

At some point, I had to accept that the scriptures were true. I had to change my theology about who God is—that He was not this domineering figure that just wanted to punish me. I had to see Him as someone who wanted to love me and care for me. Even when I mess up, His grace abounds. I don't deserve it, but He continues to give Himself in love.

Loving me the way God loves me affects everything in my life. There are times I'm having a bad day, and I can look in the mirror and say I like myself. I really like this hair. I really like this skin. I really like these lips, and I really love this lipstick on them. I can look in the mirror and be okay with who I am. Then I can move forward and be okay with every aspect of my life.

Chapter Seven
Loving Yourself

Study Verse – *"But who are you, my friend, to talk back to God? A clay pot does not ask the man who made it, 'why did you make me like this?'" Romans 9:20*

Truthfully, how often do we question God's masterpiece? God, why wasn't I taller? Why can't I play basketball? Why aren't I thinner? Why don't I have beautiful hips? Why is my hair texture like this?

In the first half of the book, we talked a lot about how God's love for us works and how it sees us through tough circumstances. However, one thing that a lot of people never acknowledge is their love-o-meter for themselves. You understand why you should love God, and you understand that He loves you. But it can be difficult to understand "why" He loves you when you don't even love yourself completely. Not having complete love for yourself doesn't necessarily mean that you have low self-esteem or you are depressed. Having complete love for yourself requires you

Perfectly Loved: Knowing Love on God's Terms

to be able to see the whole you and enjoy the sum of all your parts. It doesn't mean that there still isn't work to be done within you, but it means that you are accepting of your strengths and weaknesses. You can accept your flaws in understanding that God can and will renew them. And you accept your whole being because you acknowledge it as God's greatest masterpiece. In order to love the complete you, you must know who you are in God's eyes.

Throughout my life, I always felt like I had pretty high self-esteem. I got picked on as a child for the quirky things that I could not control. I was called a "goody two shoes," picked on for my slue feet, being vertically challenged, my inability to dance to the rhythm all black girls should be able to find, and even for my darker skin complexion. Despite the teasing, I never realized that I had any self-esteem issues. Although the jokes hurt, when I would come home my parents would build me back up again. They always reminded me of my greatness, and I had a habit of believing them over what any of the kids in school would say.

Notwithstanding all the mockery people made of me, I was always pretty popular. I attribute that to my consistent involvement in multiple activities, high grade point average, social butterfly tendencies, and loud voice. I would not be ignored, and I enjoyed and knew how to socially interact with all types of people. It wasn't until college that I actually had to face some of the things within me that highlighted the esteem issues that I had been oblivious to. This is because it wasn't until college that I actually felt ignored. It dawned on me that my constant need for acceptance from people was causing me to do things that I knew was morally and ethically wrong. I got involved in activities that I didn't even like just to be liked. If you looked at the smile on my face and my pictures, you would think I enjoyed the clubbing and the drinking. But I just enjoyed the acceptance I received from people when I did it. My need for acceptance became detrimental, because when people didn't accept me, I dealt with feelings of depression, my grades slipped slightly, and I even quit running track. I had to find myself; thankfully, God found me first.

If you're reading this book, God has caught up to you and found you as well. God wants you to know who you are to Him. In my youth, I chose to believe what my parents told me I was over what kids in school said I was. It was indelibly within me to believe the opinion of the ones I thought created me. When I started to recognize my existence as God's child, I also chose to believe what He told me I was over what I thought I needed to be in order to be accepted by others.

In this chapter we will discuss who God says we are and also learn about what God shaped us to be.

The Bible not only tells us who God is, but it gives biblical affirmations about our identity in Jesus Christ. I have listed twenty biblical affirmations and how they remind us why we are loveable and should love ourselves.

Perfectly Loved: Knowing Love on God's Terms

Biblical Affirmations of Identity

1. I am a child of God.

"But to all who believed him and accepted him, he gave the right to become children of God." John 1:12

You are a child of God. You aren't His child because of something good you have done, nor will any wrong you have done in your past keep you from being called his child. You are His child simply because you believe in His fullness, which comes by believing in His Son, Christ Jesus.

2. I am God's glory.

"Yes, I am the vine; you are the branches. Those who remain in me, and I in them, will produce much fruit. For apart from me you can do nothing." John 15:5

Vines exist with the purpose of producing fruit. The gardener who tends to the vine only receives recognition for his amazing vines when they produce fruit. In this context, Jesus is the vine and God is the gardener. The vine cannot bear fruit without the branches. Water and nutrients travel through the vine to give life to the branches so that they can bear fruit. This makes the branch extremely important to the gardener. Without the branch carrying the fruit, the gardener gets no glory. The fruit of the branch is the glory of God, which makes you, as the branch, a symbol of God's glory. Thereby, we do not necessarily live our lives for God. Rather, we allow God to live out His life through us.

3. I am a friend of Jesus

"I no longer call you slaves, because a master doesn't confide in his slaves. Now you are my friends, since I have told you everything the Father told me." John 15:15

Here, Jesus clearly defines the difference between a slave and friend to His disciples. A slave is someone with no choice or will of his or her own. Because a slave has no insight into the "why," he or she has no control over the "what." However, a friend is a confidant who is given the chance to commune with you and learn knowledge and wisdom that provides insight into the "why." A slave is given demands without a choice. A friend is given commands with a choice and the ability to make a decision. As a friend of God the choice you make is determined by the "why" that God provides. Your "why" is love. With this insight, the friend has a choice in the actions they will take.

"As branches we receive, as disciples we follow, and as friends we commune"[14]. God communes with you. He tells you His secrets, and He reveals things to you that many will never have the opportunity to hear. You are working with the knower of all things.

4. I am innocent.

"Yet God freely and graciously declares that we are righteous. He did this through Christ Jesus when he freed us from the penalty for our sins." Romans 3:24

Perfectly Loved: Knowing Love on God's Terms

God made us innocent at no cost of our own. He did it through His grace, which is His manner of acceptance and favor on us that is only made possible because Jesus paid the ransom to deliver us from our sins. He paid the price for our innocence. When you acknowledge your innocence, you can defensively combat anyone who comes against you and reminds you of your past mistakes. Who cares who they think or thought you were? Today you are redeemed. You are innocent of all charges.

5. I am no longer a slave to sin.

"We know that our old sinful selves were crucified with Christ so that sin might lose its power in our lives. We are no longer slaves to sin." Romans 6:6

Sin has no control over you. When you are faced with temptations, you control your actions through the love of Christ that is within you. When people call you a drug addict, sex addict, liar, or fiend, you can now declare to them that those sins do not control you. They have no power, because the Holy Spirit working within you has all might and control.

6. I am a part of a royal priesthood.

"But you are a chosen generation, a royal priesthood, a holy nation, His own special people, that you may proclaim the praises of Him who called you out of darkness into His marvelous light; who once were not a people but are now the people of God, who had not obtained mercy but now have obtained mercy." 1 Peter 2:9-10 (NIV)

You are chosen to be a part of a select group of chosen people. You make up the greatest of what God has created. That makes you more than ordinary. You are extraordinary.

7. I will not be condemned by God.

"So now there is no condemnation for those who belong to Christ Jesus" Romans 8:1

When someone is condemned, there is a judgment set against them. However, Jesus stands in front of you covering your sins with His love. When God sees you, He doesn't see your sins; He sees His Son. Other people cannot condemn you either. Disregard the judgments people make against you and believe what God says you are in Him.

8. I am an heir with Christ.

"And since we are his children, we are his heirs. In fact, together with Christ we are heirs of God's glory. But if we are to share his glory, we must also share his suffering." Romans 8:17

There is a distinct difference between the suffering you go through and the suffering of nonbelievers. As sons and daughters of Christ, you suffer in order to see God's glory. When you sacrifice your life and show love to others, you are suffering for God's sake. The good news is that your suffering leads to an eternal inheritance. Many people will have financial distress in their lives, but when believers have financial distress, they have the hope of God to look forward to. Even if they never become rich on earth, they are promised a one hundred-fold inheritance in heaven, and what is in heaven can never be lost. As a believer, your treasure is in heaven. I would be poor for one hundred years on earth if it meant I would be rich in eternity. Everything belongs to God, and because you are in Him, everything also belongs to you.

9. I have wisdom, righteousness, sanctification, and redemption.

"God has united you with Christ Jesus. For our benefit God made him to be wisdom itself. Christ made us right with God; he made us pure and holy, and he freed us from sin." 1 Corinthians 1:30

You are righteous, which means you are equitable in character. To have equity is to be in right standing with God so that there is no prejudice against you. You have been made of worthy value to God and sanctified by Christ. Your sanctification makes you clean and pure. You have been given a clean slate to put more of the goodness of God within you. God did all of this when Jesus redeemed you from sin by taking you in as His own.

10. My body is a temple of the Holy Spirit.

"Don't you realize that your body is the temple of the Holy Spirit, who lives in you and was given to you by God? You do not belong to yourself." 1 Corinthians 6:19

"The Temple that King Solomon built for the Lord was 90 feet long, 30 feet wide, and 45 feet high. The entry room at the front of the Temple was 30 feet wide, running across the entire width of the Temple. He built a complex of rooms against the outer walls of the Temple, all the way around the sides and rear of the building. The complex was three stories high, the bottom floor

Rhana A. Gittens

being 7 ½ feet wide, the second floor 9 feet wide, and top floor 10 ½ feet wide. The rooms were connected to the walls of the Temple by beams resting on ledges built out from the wall. There were winding stairs going up to the second floor; and another flight of stairs between the second and third floors. The entire inside, from floor to ceiling, was paneled with wood. He paneled the walls and ceilings with cedar, and he used planks of cypress for the floors. He prepared the inner sanctuary at the far end of the Temple, where the Ark of the Lord's Covenant would be placed. This inner sanctuary was 30 feet high. He overlaid the inside with solid gold. He decorated all the walls of the inner sanctuary and the main room with carvings of cherubim, palm trees, and open flowers. He overlaid the floor in both rooms with gold. It took seven years to build the Temple." (1 Kings 6:2-3, 5-6, 8, 15, 19-21, 29-30, 38)

  The material building of the Temple of God no longer exists. As a New Testament believer, you are now His Temple. When you see how much work God put into the physical building, imagine how much work He is putting into you. Solomon got cedars from Lebanon, a labor force of thirty thousand men from all of Israel, seventy thousand common laborers, eighty thousand quarry workers, thirty-six hundred supervisors, and hired the most skilled and talented interior decorator from Tyre to set up the interior furnishings. Today Jesus has the entire world working to build you up as a holy Temple. Our perfect God orchestrates specific networks, locations, people, places, and timing to get you exactly where you are supposed to be when you are supposed to be there just to make you into the perfect you for all of Him. He only wants to dwell inside the very best.

Your body is so precious to God. Its beauty comes from the Holy Spirit that dwells within it. When people see the God within you, they will say, "There is something different about you." You are absolutely beautiful and handsome. I had to learn that too, because people would have me to think that dark complexions aren't pretty enough. But then I was reminded, "I was created by the best artist in the world. How could you ever call my God's creation ugly? My God is amazing, and He made no mistakes on me. I'm beautiful because God loves looking at me. He calls me His."

11. I am one with all who are in Christ.

"There is no longer Jew or Gentile, slave or free, male and female. For you are all one in Christ Jesus." Galatians 3:28

In God there is no one greater than any other. Black, White, Hispanic, Asian, male, female, rich, or poor—all go to heaven or hell the same way. When you are a believer in Christ, you are a part of one body. In this body, there are no color lines. We are all brothers and sisters, and we all have the same mission: to bring Christ's love to the entire world. You are a part of something that does not segregate you or put you beneath anyone else. In fact, without you, the body of Christ is missing a very important piece. You are not more or less important; you are equally important in the body of Christ.

12. I have been blessed with every spiritual blessing.

"All praise to God, the Father of our Lord Jesus Christ, who has blessed us with every spiritual blessing in the heavenly realms because we are united with Christ." Ephesians 1:3 (NIV)

What are the spiritual blessings that God has blessed you with? In Christ, you are blessed with forgiveness, wisdom and insight, communion with God, the fruits of the Spirit, power to complete His mission on the earth, hope in your future, and life as His child[15]. These blessings are greater than any present anyone can buy you. Why? Because they cannot be bought. They are completely free when you believe; further, they can never be lost, and only God can give them. While new dresses, shoes, trips, televisions, and cars can be purchased and then lost, repossessed, ripped, broken, or stolen, God's blessings can never be taken away. These are gifts in which you can boast, because God chose you in advance to receive them.

13. I was specifically chosen by God to be His child.

"God decided in advance to adopt us into his own family by bringing us to himself through Jesus Christ. This is what he wanted to do and it gave him great pleasure." Ephesians 1:4

God thought of you before your parents were conceived. He knew you before the creation of the universe, and He already knew you would be adopted into His family through Christ. He predestined you for this journey. That makes you special. Everyone is not chosen, but those who are called and decide to answer the call are accepted into a family that is unwavering. God is so happy to have you with Him. Your company in His family brings Him joy, and if He were to ever lose you, He would travel high and low and go through fire and water to get you back. If the entire world was perfect and you were the only person who needed Jesus to save them, Jesus still would have died on the cross just for you. He didn't die to save millions. He died to save you.

14. I am a citizen of heaven.

"But we are citizens of heaven, where the Lord Jesus Christ lives. And we are eagerly waiting for him to return as our Savior." Philippians 3:20

Your ticket to heaven is guaranteed when you believe that Christ died and rose again for your sins. Jesus paid your airfare. As a citizen of heaven, you have all the rights to the glory of God that awaits you there. In fact, Jesus is in heaven setting up a place for you (John 14:3). Sometimes I get through my roughest days on earth by thinking about what my mansion in heaven may look like. I want to do the right things down here so that I have all things I love when I get up there. When I went to Paris, I had the most delectable French Vanilla and strawberry crepe. So now I always imagine that heaven for me will just be me, Jesus, and a crepe. I live out every day excited for the moment when Jesus and I can eat that crepe together. But then I remember that when I sat down at that little bistro in Paris, Jesus was with me. He gives me heaven on earth when I just take the time to notice His presence in everything I do. We eat together all the time, and you eat with Him too.

15. I am God's masterpiece.

"For we are God's masterpiece. He has created us anew in Christ Jesus, so we can do the good things He planned for us long ago." Ephesians 2:10

You are a masterpiece created by the master Himself. Your beauty outweighs any of God's other creations. Your power and abilities can move mountains if you just believe. The *Mona Lisa* and thousands of other artworks present in the Louvre cannot compare to the masterpiece that is you. Who could fashion a heartbeat to pulse in perfect rhythmic timing to push the nutrients through your blood to every living organ within your body? Take a look at your hands, feet, legs, and arms. What human being could imagine such a magnificent creation as you? There is nothing inferior about you.

16. I am a light in the Lord.

"For once you were full of darkness, but now you have light from the Lord. So live as people of light!" Ephesians 5:8

How do people of light live? Maybe we should compare ourselves to fireflies. Firefly lights are the most efficient lights in the world—100 percent of their energy is emitted as light. In comparison, an incandescent bulb only emits 10 percent of its energy as light. Fireflies are characterized by some other special abilities. They communicate with each other through light, their baby eggs glow, they are found on almost every continent, they are medically useful, and their bad taste keeps predators away[16]. It's not a coincidence that people who are the light of the Lord have the same awe-striking abilities as fireflies.

As the light of God, you are able to communicate to others with your light, which is the love of God. In addition, your children glow too because of your light. God has given you the ability to spread His Word to the entire world and be present everywhere. You are also useful to people on the earth because of the power of your Spiritual gifts to heal and set them free. Finally, the devil hates the taste of you. You are so protected and strong in the Word that the devil doesn't even want to deal with you. Be a firefly.

17. God loves me and has chosen me.
"We know, dear brothers and sisters, that God loves you and has chosen you to be his own people." 1 Thessalonians 1:4

Despite what anyone else thinks or says about you, God loves you. He chose you. You are His.

18. I am the apple of His eye.
"Whoever touches you touches the apple of his eye." Zechariah 2:8 (NIV)

God protects you because you are His most precious procession. When people harm you, it is as if they are harming Jesus. You are an extension of Him on the earth. You are the apple of His eye.

Rhana A. Gittens

19. I am a member of Christ's body.

"No one hates his own body, but feeds and cares for it, just as Christ cares for the church. And we are members of his body." Ephesians 5:29-30

You are a piece of Christ Himself on the earth. You carry Christ with you everywhere you go. Therefore, Christ protects you as He would protect His own body. If you were Christ's legs, necessary to carry the Word of God to far places, He will keep you strong and able. If you are Christ's mouthpiece, necessary to teach and preach the Word of God, He will keep your thoughts pure. God watches over His mission and the members of His body that have been created to perform His mission on the earth. You are partaking in the promise of God.

20. I have been made complete in Christ.

"So you also are complete through your union with Christ, who is the head over every ruler and authority." Colossians 2:10

So what is it that makes you complete? In order to love the full you, you must finally recognize affirmation #20. You are complete because of Christ Jesus. Before Christ, you were only a partial image of yourself working at a devastatingly lower altitude of what you were called to. If you thought you were great before Christ, then you haven't even scratched the surface of your propensity. If you thought you were weak before Christ, you haven't begun to imagine your predisposed strength. It is by the power of God that we are shaped into His image in order to garner

Perfectly Loved: Knowing Love on God's Terms

His glory. We are loveable simply because He said so, and we can love ourselves simply because He loves us.

Pastor Rick Warren of Saddleback Church in California teaches the concept of SHAPE in His book *The Purpose Driven Life*. Your **s**piritual gifts, **h**eart's desires, **a**bilities, **p**ersonality, and **e**xperiences create your SHAPE[17]. These five aspects make you beautifully unique and a necessary member of Christ's body. God knew what He was shaping you to be before you were ever born. Psalm 139:13(MSG) says, "You shaped me first inside, then out, you formed me in my mother's womb."

Your spiritual gifts provide an ability that is given by the Holy Spirit and only available to believers. Every believer has at least one spiritual gift, and there is no spiritual gift given to everyone. Some gifts include wisdom, knowledge, faith, healing, miracles, prophecy, discernment, tongues, interpretation of tongues, teaching, apostleship, helping, and leadership. (For further information regarding spiritual gifts, see 1 Corinthians 12-14). What makes spiritual gifts unique from anything else you can ever receive is that they are completely free, and all you have to do is believe in them and your power to wield them. When you wield spiritual gifts for the benefit of others, you become the fruit of God. Your heart's desires provide the motivation for your use of your God given gifts for His glory.

The heart portion of your being explores your motivation for the things you do. It deciphers the reasoning behind your goals. Your heart's desires make you unique, because you could be moving toward the same goal as four other people but have a

Rhana A. Gittens

completely different reason for it. The motivation behind the goal will define how it is accomplished and whether it is successful. For instance, you may want to open a nonprofit organization to mentor young men specifically because you want to see young boys get graduate-level degrees. However, other people may want to mentor young men because they grew up without a father and want to focus on fatherless boys, have seen trouble for inner-city men and want to break the cycle of incarceration, or you love athletics and believe that sports and arts in school give boys positive self-esteem. Your hearts desires can be good or bad. Psalm 37:4 says, "Take delight in the Lord, and He will give you your heart's desires." This verse does not describe God as a candy-giver; rather, it insures that God will change your heart to desire a specific kind of candy. Therefore, God will provide specific experiences, abilities, and personality traits to insure that your motivations for your goals are in line with the purpose He has for your life.

    Rick Warren describes your abilities as the natural talents you were born with. Based on your heart's desires, your abilities can be used for good or bad[18]. But just like your spiritual gifts, your natural abilities should be used for God's glory. There are numerous specialized abilities (listed in the Think About It section of this chapter). They are skills that you are just born with. As a baby, Dominique Moceanu's (1996 Olympic gold medalist in gymnastics) parents let her hang from a clothing line as a toddler to test her strength and see if she had a natural talent for gymnastics. When she was able to keep herself up, her parents had her trained by Romanian power couple Bela and Marta Karolyi[19]. She was born to be a gymnast. In addition, skills are interchangeable, meaning they can be used for numerous activities. Moceanu's upper body strength could have been used toward swimming, weight lifting, or even shipping and delivering heavy packages. Your personality, experiences, and heart's desires will affect how you will use your abilities.

Similarly, each of us has an extremely unique personality. Differing personalities are often easily identifiable when you work in a team. In Christian ministries, you may put together twenty of your church members to lead the singles ministry because they are single and they seem to be dedicated members of the church body. However, those two characteristics about them in no way define how that group will work together, because each of those twenty people will have distinct personality traits. Some are introverts and others extroverts. Some will be emotionally driven by their feelings and the feelings of others, while some will be rational thinkers. There will also be people who will state their point through their actions, and others will voice their opinion. The best part of working in God's kingdom is that there is no right or wrong personality for God. Jesus Himself showed a myriad of personalities depending on the situation. At times He was straight-forward and informative (Mark 9:29), other times He was spoke in parables (Matthew 25:14-30). But when He had to be He was solemn and even cried for the loss of friends (John 11:35). He was sensitive when He spoke to some (John 4:19-29) and strong (Luke 11:38-42) when He spoke to others. He was also funny and sarcastic (Matthew 22:20-22), but He wasn't afraid to show His anger like when He flipped the tables when He saw people trading money in the holy Temple (Matthew 21:12). Jesus's use of various personalities should make you proud of your own unique combination of traits that make you who you are.

While you are born with your abilities and God gives you your spiritual gifts, experiences are often beyond your control, but they allow God to mold you for your specific purpose. In order to truly see the full you, you must examine your experiences. Some kinds of experiences that are worth examining are family experiences, educational experiences, vocational experiences, spiritual experiences, ministry experiences, and painful experiences[20]. Although some experiences may bring happiness and others cause hurt, they all work together to create the perfect you. "The very experiences that you have resented or regretted most in life—the ones you've wanted to hide and forget—are the experiences God wants to use to help others. They are your ministry!" says Warren.

Your SHAPE is a way to identify who you are in completion. You will be able to love yourself completely, once you have identified your SHAPE and accepted the powerful affirmations of who God says you are. God doesn't love a partial you, He loves a full you, because He knows all of who you are. You should get to know yourself as well.

Perfectly Loved: Knowing Love on God's Terms

Think About It

1. **What abilities do you feel you have? Circle your abilities. Feel free to add any that you do not see here.**

entertain	encourage	n u m e r i c a l
motivate	teach	expertise
question/interview	write	classify
research	advertise	welcome
conceptualize art	fix/restore	customer service
analyze	cook	decorate
plan	remember	garden
manage	operate machinery	
counsel		

2. **Analyze your experiences**

Family Experiences – How is your family set up, and how do you interact with your family?

_____
_____
_____
_____

Spiritual experiences – List and describe some meaningful moments you have had with God.

_____
_____

Rhana A. Gittens

_____
_____

Educational/Vocational Experiences – What were your favorite subjects in school? What valuable skills have you learned from your work experiences?

_____
_____
_____
_____

Ministry Experiences – What ministries have you been a part of? If none yet, what ministries would you consider joining?

_____
_____
_____
_____

Painful Experiences – What hurtful experiences from your past have taught you valuable lessons?

_____
_____
_____
_____

MY STORY – MAKEDA

My cousin had four kids, and her first was born when she was just seventeen. She was always super smart, and my family thought she ruined her life after she had her first child. Things got a lot harder for her, and the more children she had, the harder it got. On the outside, people saw her as being on the "wrong path" and me being on the "right path." I was in college, and she was raising kids. Despite that, I believe she blessed me much more than I blessed her. When she got sick with cancer, she became very close to God. At the time, I wasn't as close to my faith. She would text me, and at the end of each text would be a confirmation of God's love for me. She was teaching me much more than a textbook ever could. She taught me that if God could forgive her for her mistakes and love her unconditionally, then He would do that for me. I realized I can't have expectations for my family and judge them based on what I think is the right thing for them to be doing. Despite their mistakes, God loves them.

Overtime I became strong in my faith, and I changed. I learned God's love for me and strived to be a better person. But I realized my family hadn't progressed at my same pace.

Don't get me wrong. My family knows God, but our family's culture encourages honesty and sometimes that honesty comes to a point of extreme bluntness that turns into arguments. There are times that I feel like there is a battle between the way the Lord wants us to respond to circumstances and the way my family expects us to respond. I remember one argument I got in with my mother. Although she was proud of my progress with the Lord, in this one situation she seemed to forget all of that. Initially I responded appropriately but eventually my patience ran thin. I was angry not because of the argument but because I was pushed into a

Rhana A. Gittens

reaction... pushed into being the person I fought so hard to get rid of. I was disappointed because my number one supporter and believer in my progression had put me in the last place I'd ever want to be. After I forgave myself, forgave my mother, and took time for reflection, I realized that now that I had Christ, I had the credibility to share with my family how God wants us to love on each other even when we may not think someone in our family is making the right decision. The devil tries to set up the perfect situation to get you to buckle, but the Lord uses that same situation to test you, and He wants you to come out like an undefeated warrior. Not everything will be perfect, but you have to analyze it and learn from it. That's what makes you a good follower of Christ. Had my mother and I handled the situation differently, we could have been an example for the younger generation of our family. The arguments and disagreements are just a way for the devil to divide us.

    Over the years, I have also learned that I have to be patient with my family. Everything happens in God's timing. I have to remember that God is in control, like in the situation with my mommy. I love my mother so much I just wanted to let out my thoughts so we could move past it. When I asked her if she was ready to talk about it, she responded "no". I was bothered because I knew she wouldn't let me know when she was ready, but I knew that to be effective, I had to bite my tongue, take a step back, be patient and continue to show her love. Two days later, she got on the phone with me talking about a completely different topic, and as the conversation continued we unexpectedly started talking about our previous argument. It was perfect timing for her, because she had been reading her prayer book that day. God planned it perfectly so that her heart was open to hear from me.

People are very complex, and there is no way to understand every aspect of a person's personality. However, I can't continue to think people will never change. God is powerful. He can do anything. I have hope that my family will grow in Christ and I have acted on that hope by planting seeds, praying for them and bringing up God in the conversation when I can.

For me, family is duty. God provided me with these people to call family, to encourage them and take care of them. If I want the world to be a better place, I have to start with my family. I owe it to them and I owe it to God.

Rhana A. Gittens

Chapter Eight
Loving in Family

Study Verse– *"For we are not fighting against flesh-and-blood enemies, but against evil rulers and authorities of the unseen world, against mighty powers in the dark world, and against evil spirits in the heavenly places." Ephesians 6:12*

I haven't always loved my family the way I should. The sin I regret the most was my ability to love, forgive, and do for others —except my family. The people who have loved me and cared for me from the very first day I was put on this earth have often been the hardest for me to forgive. More often than not, I took their love for granted. I never had to doubt the love of my family toward me. I never questioned it, because it was always obvious. Both of my parents sacrificed their lives, time, dreams, and money to raise my brother and me and make sure our dreams came to fruition. Although I communicated with my parents every day after I left for college, I did not truly let them into my world. I didn't communicate all the ins and outs of my life, and for a while I'm sure that they felt like they didn't know me much anymore. As I matured, I realized that all my parents ever wanted was to share my life with me. That is what love meant to them. Yes, they could call me when they needed something and I was always there; but giving things is not giving love. Giving love is a giving of you in one of the most unselfish ways. It is sharing your Spirit with someone else so that they can truly feel the love that dwells within you. We must not forget to give that love to our families.

The family, beginning with marriage, is God's first and most important ministry. God created the marriage ministry of Adam and Eve, and then they bared children, which created the very first family. Before there were young adult ministries, children's ministries, worship ministries, etc., there was the family ministry. Through the family, all other ministries are birthed. Wives and husbands, as a picture of Christ's relationship with the Church, are to instill God's love and Word in their children. Women and men are expected to train the youth and encourage them to live honorably. The guardians and parents of children within the family help them to understand their gifts, how to treat others, and assist them in following their God-given purposes. Therefore, when we have strong families, we build strong churches and strong ministries.

Family is to be an earthly representation of how God loves the church. People get tripped up because they build up their church ministries, careers, and friend relationships; but when they come home, their houses are in shackles. Your family is where it all begins, and it is the root from which all your other interactions stem. When your home is crippled, it will come out one way or another in all the other ministries and relationships you touch. "For if a man cannot manage his own household, how can he take care of God's church?" (1 Timothy 3:5).

Rhana A. Gittens

Because the family is the centerpiece of God's ministry on the earth, the devil attacks family first. According to the Center for Disease Control and Prevention, only half of first marriages actually survive twenty years[21]. In 2012, 40.7 percent of all births in the United States were to unmarried women. That is 1,609,619 children born out of wedlock in the United States within twelve months[22].

Marriage is deeper than companionship. The stability, strength, and longevity of marriage creates healthy Christian families. When we pray for healthy Christian marriages and Christian children, we are praying for the repairing of God's first ministry. When the family is destroyed, Satan has a party. When we think of the following facts, there is no reason to not see why the devil attacks families first:

- 31 percent of youth with divorced parents dropped out of high school, and 37 percent of youth born to unwed mothers dropped out of high school[23].

- 33 percent of daughters with divorced parents had a teen pregnancy, and 37 percent of daughters born to unwed mothers had teen pregnancy[24].

- Children in high-conflict households experience many of the same problems as do children with divorced parents[25].

- Children living with cohabiting biological parents, compared with children living with continuously married parents, had more behavioral problems, more emotional problems, and lower levels of school engagement (that is, caring about school and doing homework) [26].

Of course, the statistics above do not describe all families, nor do they imply reasons for the many issues in people's lives that can cause divorce or pregnancy out of wedlock. However, they do serve to describe some of the problems that we see in today's families and show that when the devil attacks families, he destroys lives.

Even when we think of the slavery of the African people in America, we see how slavery, among other things, caused a destruction of the black family. Slavery inhibited family formation, because enslaved people were not able to legally marry, and families were split apart by having separate slave masters and the selling off of the family members to different owners[27]. The events of the past perpetuated a decrease in the paternal parent in African American households today and stand to reason why there is a lack of black men as heads of households today. If the devil can destroy the family within a race of people, he can also destroy an entire people if no repairing is done.

The facts above are simply in place to showcase the importance of family and demonstrate how the destruction of family has a snowball effect on future generations of cultural groups and family lineages. Therefore, it is the job of Christians, with a heart of love, to instill love in the family and keep this ministry afloat, for it is the beginning of God's exemplification of love for other people on the earth. Evangelism and dispersion of love begins at home.

Rhana A. Gittens

Withstanding the devil's attacks on your family

In order to withstand the devil's attacks on our families, we can study our biblical ancestors' testimonies. They didn't always get it right, but we can learn from their mistakes.

The first family, Adam and Eve and their two sons, were attacked by jealousy. Cain was intensely jealous of his younger brother, Abel, because God accepted Abel's gift to the Lord but did not accept his own. God accepted Abel's gift because he gave the very best lamb from his flock, while Cain just gave the Lord any old crops from the field, with little acknowledgement to bring the Lord his very best. In his anger and jealousy, Cain killed his brother (Genesis 4).

From Cain and Abel's story we learn that one of the biggest attacks of the enemy comes when people are offended[28]. Cain was offended that God did not accept his gift. His offense turned into jealousy against his brother, and his anger ended in murder. In order to combat the menace of offense in our lives, we must soften our hearts. Sin causes our hearts to be hardened and love to be void. God will put you through trials and afflictions in order to refine you and allow you to see the areas where your heart has been hardened. Your trials will inevitably work to soften your heart so that attacks of offense cannot grow into bitterness, anger, and resentment within you. Furthermore, when we are able to see the truth in ourselves, we are freed from deception, and we stop seeing ourselves as victims and blaming others who have hurt us[29]. Cain was unable to see that his lack of sacrificial giving was the reason God did not accept his gift. If he could have seen that, he would not have felt victimized and blamed his brother. "Why do you look at the speck of sawdust in your brother's eye and pay no attention to the plank in your own eye?" (Matthew 7:3). Make sure you are not the Cain of your family.

The next family to review is that of Abraham's nephew, Lot. The evil in Lot's family shows the attack of sexual immorality that can cause the destruction of love within a family. Genesis 19:1-8 recounts the story of how Lot offered his daughters to rapists. Before Lot's home of Sodom was destroyed, two angels disguised as men came to Lot's home as guests. The deplorable men of Sodom saw the two guests come in to the home. They surrounded the house and demanded that Lot give them up so that they could have sex with them. Lot refused to offer up the men. Unfortunately, Lot offered his daughters in their stead. However, the angels stepped in, grabbed Lot, and pulled him into the house and bolted the door. Lot's daughters were not harmed.

When reading this story with modern eyes, it's considered unthinkable to offer your daughters up for rape. Unfortunately, sexual exploitation occurs in families in multiple forms all the time. According to the National Sexual Violence Resource Center, 17 million children will be abused over the next eighteen years, 90 percent of molested children know their abuser, and 93 percent of child molesters consider themselves religious[30].

Rhana A. Gittens

These situations in families reveal sin and how much sin can be absorbed into your family. However, like in Lot's family, these situations also give God's angels and workers a chance to work. God will destroy sin. If you are the person in the family to whom it has been revealed that sin is there, you are also the one who invites love into the home. You pray for the family, and you get them help. God will destroy the evil and protect the innocent in His timing. Lot opened the door for the angels, and they protected him from the destruction that he didn't even know was coming. It was because of Abraham's prayers to God to protect Lot's family that the angels showed up to his door that night. Are you ready to make yourself available to be the praying Abraham in your family?

As a further example of attacks on families, the family of siblings Mary, Martha, and Lazarus were attacked with illness in their home. John 11 reveals the story of Lazarus's illness. Mary and Martha went to Jesus and let Him know that His friend Lazarus was sick and beckoned Him to come to Judea to help. Jesus responded, "Lazarus's sickness will not end in death. No, it happened for the glory of God so that the Son of God will receive glory from this." When Jesus arrived at Judea, He was told that Lazarus had already been in the grave for four days. Martha and Mary were very upset with Jesus for not coming sooner. Jesus went to the tomb and said, "Didn't I tell you that you would see God's glory if you believe?" Then He shouted, "Lazarus, come out!" And Lazarus awoke.

The devil attacks our families by getting people to waver in their faith. Doubt often turns into complete disbelief, which causes us to be separated from God. All trials in life are for God's glory. Even if Lazarus was to have died and Jesus to have never brought him back, God would have still been glorified. God is glorified by our faith in His love. When illness and financial distress attempt to cripple our families, it is our faith in God's love that sees us through. We must remember that no matter the outcome, God is faithful to His promise that all things will work together for the good of those who love the Lord (Roman 8:28). Therefore, even though situations in your family may look like death, we must have faith in the fact that Jesus is "the way, the truth, and the life" (John 14:6). Anyone who believes in Him will live even after dying. Are you able to identify the person with unwavering faith in your family? Are you that person?

Even when looking at my life, I see the attack the devil places on my own family. He doesn't always attack me face-to-face. What I mean by that is that the devil doesn't always come after my body with illness or my bank account with financial insult. Rather, in my own life the devil has attacked me by attacking my family members with illness, financial distress, and separation. In my immaturity while I was in college, I thought that if I separated my heart from my family's pain, it couldn't touch me. When things went wrong, I didn't really want my parents to tell me about it. I wanted to be treated like the baby and shielded from all the troubles within my family unit.

But when I matured and made a relationship with God, I realized that separating my heart from my family was breaking their hearts. In addition, even more detrimental was that the separation of me from them spiritually was keeping them from reaping any of the blessings that were being bestowed upon me. When I finally tied my spirit back to the spirit and soul of my family unit, I was blessed in order to bless them, and the bad that I was running from started to be filled with the good of Jesus Christ that began to flourish in my household.

Loving your first ministry- Family

Let's be real. Sometimes it is really hard to love your family. It's hard because there are times when you just don't like them. I completely understand that feeling. But more importantly, God completely understands that feeling. Regardless of those struggles, our families, no matter what form they come in, are God's gift to us. Whether your family is all blood relatives or you have an adopted family of guardians and friends, these love principles still apply. God is able to love us despite who we are, because He is able to see the good in us. He does not love us based on who we are without Him but who we will be with Him.

We must, therefore, do the same with our families. We have to find the good in our family. You may find good attributes in every member of your family. Even more, you may be able to visualize the good they can become once God's love enters their hearts. If there is any ounce of good left for salvation in your family, God considers it a family worth protecting (Genesis 18:22-33). And if that family is worth protecting, is it not worth it to you to continue to show love to all within it so that the devil's attacks can be combated?

First you must check yourself. Are you harboring a feeling of offense for someone in your family? Has that offense grown into bitterness, anger, and jealousy? In order to relieve yourself of the offense, you must forgive. Clear your heart of any impurities that are keeping you from having love, hope, joy, and faith. Pray that God gives you a spirit of love and forgiveness so that you can reconcile and be the demonstration of love within your family.

Secondly, pray fervently for your family and ask for outside help and counsel when you need it. In order to protect your family against the enemy, you have to pray against the enemy. We are all too often fighting the members of our families, and they are not the true enemy. We do not battle flesh and blood, but we battle the evil spirits, authorities, and wickedness that lie within them (Ephesians 6:12). In order to battle evil Spirits, you have to have a spiritual prayer life. Stop arguing, cursing, and fighting with your family. Your verbal attacks on them will not clean up the situation. Your verbal attack on the devil with the use of God's Word is the only thing that can free your family from any demonic controls that may lie there. When you actually are speaking to your family, you should speak with love and kindness, because you get a whole lot more sugar with honey.

Finally, have faith in God's love for your family. Encourage your family members through the struggles of their life. You must remind them of God's faithfulness and give them hope. In addition, praise them when they succeed. Share in their laughter and their tears.

Rhana A. Gittens

The last chapter of the book of Ephesians begins with, "Children, obey your parents, because you belong to the Lord, for this the right thing to do. 'Honor your father and mother.' This is the first commandment with a promise: If you honor your father and mother, 'things will go well for you, and you will have a long life on earth'" (Ephesians 6:1-2). You obey your parents because you belong to God. You don't obey them because you agree with them. You abide by them simply because God told you to, and you are His, and your parents are the authority God placed on the earth for you. As long as your parents do not provoke you to do evil or sin, you are expected to do what they say. Honoring your parents does not stop with adulthood. As you grow into adulthood you learn to continue to honor them with love.

Further in Ephesians 6, parents are beckoned to not provoke their children to anger by the way they treat them. "Rather, bring them up with the discipline and instruction that comes from the Lord" (Ephesians 6:4). If children obey the principle to honor and parents obey the principle of discipline, families will work as God first designed.

I do not think it is by chance that Paul started Ephesians 6 with instructions for families and ended with instructions for battling the devil. The devil's strategy is to attack the family so that honor and godly discipline are corrupted. Paul reminds believers again that in order to keep a loving family, you must be ready to go to battle. I have given you practical instructions on how to defend yourself, but now let's have our families get ready for battle by putting on the full armor of God that Paul describes in Ephesians 6:10-20.

> *"Be strong in the Lord and in his mighty power. Put on all of God's armor so that you will be able to stand firm against all strategies of the devil. For we are not fighting against flesh-and-blood enemies, but against evil rulers and authorities of the unseen world, against mighty powers in this dark world, and against evil spirits in the heavenly places.*
>
> *Therefore, put on every piece of God's armor so you will be able to resist the enemy in the time of evil. Then after the battle you will still be standing firm. Stand your ground putting on the belt of truth and the body armor of God's righteousness. For shoes, put on the peace that comes from the Good News so that you will be fully prepared. In addition to all of these, hold up the shield of faith to stop the fiery arrows of the devil. Put on salvation as your helmet, and take the sword of the Spirit, which is the word of God.*
>
> *Pray in the Spirit at all times and on every occasion. Stay alert and be persistent in your prayers for all believers everywhere."*

The battle armor for your family:

- **The belt of truth** should be used to fight the lies the devil will throw at you. The belt of truth comes by reading and knowing God's truth.

- The enemy attempts to affect your emotions by making you distrust yourself and your family and lose self-worth. God's righteousness comes to you when you believe in His Son. **The breastplate of righteousness** protects you from the enemy's attacks on your heart.

- The enemy attempts to keep the gospel of Jesus Christ from coming into your family so that some of your family members will never know truth or have righteousness. You must put on **shoes that are shod with the peace that comes from the Good News** so that you are motivated to continue to speak the truth to your family.

- The devil tries to throw fiery darts of fear, doubt, and disbelief at us. When we have **the shield of faith** those darts cannot penetrate.

- When we believe in God's Son, we are saved. **The helmet of salvation** protects our mind from the devils arrows.

- The Word of God is stronger than any two-edged sword. It is the only offensive weapon of armor. We will score goals in this battle when we speak the Word of God to knock out the devil's lies. Only **the sword of the Word of God** has power against the devil.

When we decide to stand against the devil's attacks on our families, we switch our feelings of anger, jealousy, distrust, and bitterness from our family members to the devil himself. When you understand who your true enemy is, you are better able to genuinely and fervently love the family God has given you.

Perfectly Loved: Knowing Love on God's Terms

Choose today not to fight your family. Choose today to forgive, to pray, and to have faith as you turn your anger away from the people you should love and protect first.

Think About It

1. **Is there a praying Abraham in your family who is consistently praying for the protection and blessings over your family? Yes or No.** _____

2. **If there is, identify them by name.**
   _____

3. **Write a prayer for the praying Abraham in your family.**
   _____
   _____
   _____
   _____
   _____

4. **If you were unable to identify a praying Abraham for your family today, write a prayer of your own for your family as you become a praying Abraham.**
   _____
   _____
   _____
   _____

5. What blessings are you having faith in God for on behalf of your family?

_____
_____
_____
_____

6. Have you been offended by anyone in your family? List their names here.

   a. _____
   b. _____
   c. _____

7. Now, take the blessing you listed in the previous questions and pray for those same blessings over the lives of those who have offended you.

_____
_____
_____
_____

MY STORY – MELISSA

One of my coworkers was getting married. She came to work one day extremely upset and frustrated with her bridesmaid because she wasn't showing excitement about the forthcoming nuptials. My coworker was ready to remove her from the wedding completely.

I immediately advocated on the bridesmaid's behalf, saying "Well, maybe your bridesmaid has been going through some issues in her own life. Did you call her?"

Then I wondered why it was so easy for me take the bridesmaid's side. I realized I knew what the bridesmaid was going through because I had been that bridesmaid, and I lived that situation. It's crazy when God presents you with someone else's problem and suddenly it's a mirror of your own.

While I was teaching her the bridesmaid's perspective, God was teaching me the bride's perspective. I had to remind myself that before attacking the other person I needed to think about what I was doing wrong. Above all else, I too, needed self-reflection.

Sometimes it comes to the point where the bridesmaid may have to ask the bride, "Have I hurt you?" Asking that question sucks when you feel like you've been a great friend. But sometimes when you are in a season of anger and your friend is being blessed, you cannot even see how you may be offending them. But God's love requires you to see yourself and see others too.

There have been seasons where I've been caught up in my own problems, and I haven't been a good friend. In order to be a better friend, I had to learn not to take out my issues on other people who were there to support me. They couldn't walk in my shoes, but I couldn't downgrade the hurt that they felt when I was hurting.

Despite what I may be going through, I have a duty to be a good friend. When God places you in someone's life, you should want to honor God with that relationship. That means you are required to encourage your friend. I realize I am going to have friends where my complete job in their life is to get them to their purpose, and they may not be doing that same thing for me. But that's not important. God's love reminds me that when I help a friend move into their God given purpose, He will help me move into mine.

It took a while, but through the ups-and-downs I have experienced in friendships, I've realized that the one defining trait that separates a friend from an acquaintance is the spiritual bond that is created. I cannot take that spiritual bond lightly. God loves unconditionally. In the same way, I have no right to walk out on a friendship. The relationship may change over time, but the spiritual connection never ends. We have to maintain the same loving relationship with friends as God maintains with us.

Chapter Nine

Loving in Friendship

Study Verse - *"Love never gives up, never loses faith, is always hopeful, and endures through every circumstance."*

1 Corinthians 13:7

At the time of this writing I have more than 1,312 friends on Facebook. Pew Research Center data from 2014 states that half of all adult Facebook users have more than 200 friends in their network, and 15 percent of users have more than 500 friends[31]. I am a part of that 15 percent. But the bad part of my unwieldy statistic is that of the 1,312 friends I have on Facebook, I interact with less than thirty of them on a regular basis (at least twice per month). That means less than 2 percent of my Facebook friends are actually more than acquaintances or people I was close to in the past but have lost connection with. If you do the math for yourself, you may notice the same trend.

In the twenty-first century, relationships have become a short aspiration of what they were before the digital boom.

Thankfully, I am old enough to remember a time before Facebook. Although you may not have had as many "friends" before the year 2000, I believe the niche group of friend connections birthed before the digital era was stronger and more real. You knew who your true friends were because you had to go out of your way to talk to them. And when I say "go out of your way," I mean that you actually had to pick up the phone and call them, leave a voicemail, and stop by their house. When I was a kid, a random drop-by at someone's house wasn't out of the ordinary, because you weren't able to pick up your cell phone to text, "hey, I'm in the neighborhood can I drop by?" Instead, you literally just dropped by.

Today people text more than they speak, or use video conference tools more than they actually see people in person. Many relationships are exclusively online, and people see a brand of a person rather than who that person really is. We are okay with just knowing who that person is by what they put online, and relationships often die when you find out that they are a totally different person face-to-face. So in this digital age, when making a friend is more like reading a Facebook profile, sending a friend request, and clicking "like" on a status, how do we hold on to the true friendships that we have, and how do we define them?

Oftentimes we are faced with deciding who our true friends are and who is worthy of our friendship. Inevitably, we should show love to all as God proclaims, but everyone is not a friend in the God-given definition of the term. I lose a couple friends every year and gain about two-fold that many every year as well. So

Perfectly Loved: Knowing Love on God's Terms

when I lose one, I gain four; but of the new four in my life, who is really going to last? Then I have to wonder, do I have a high turnover rate for friendships? And am I the problem, or are they the problem? I consider myself blessed because I have had the same best friend since I was twelve years old. But does she just deal with me, or am I truly a good friend? And if I am a good friend to her, am I being a good friend to the other 1,311 people on my Facebook friend list? These questions can go on for days.

Regardless, my loss and gain of friends has taught me one valuable lesson: all my trust needs to be to God, and through my trust in God He will provide godly friendships. I have been blessed with friends who have truly exemplified the relationship I believe God ordained in the term "friendship." Minister Courtney Harkness of Destiny Metropolitan Worship Church states, "You don't measure the depth of your friendship by the good time you share, but by the tough times you endure. In fact, you become a friend when you have every reason to stop being someone's friend, but you don't"[32]. Furthermore, you know you are being an unconditional friend when you have gone through everything that's designed to tear the friendship apart and decide to stay the course.

In the Bible, you will find that God has placed a very large expectation and calling on friendship. In order to provide the friendship that God expresses we should have for our neighbors, we need to study God's word.

Rhana A. Gittens

Characteristics of a Friend

The relationship between Jonathan and David in the Old Testament (1 Samuel 18-31) provides a perfect example of how God shows His love for us through the friendships He provides. Jonathan and David declared themselves best friends under God, and their relationship provides four characteristics of a friend ordained by God. This chapter will describe the relationship of friendship with the example that Jonathan and David set.

1. A Friend is Loyal

Jonathan was the son of King Saul. However, his father was extremely jealous of David because the Israelites praised David as the hero above the King himself. They would sing, "Saul has killed his thousands, and David his ten thousands" (1 Samuel 18:7). It was a known fact that Saul wanted David dead. However, Jonathan loved David as his best friend and vowed to protect him against his father. He made a solemn pact with David saying, "May the Lord destroy all your enemies" (1 Samuel 18:16).

Jonathan was the epitome of loyalty. He warned David of his father's plans to destroy him, and he provided David a means to escape the king's wrath. Although Jonathan was the son of Saul, Jonathan knew God's will, and he knew right from wrong. He protected his vow to David knowing that his father would be unhappy with him.

You should also be a loyal, truthful, and honest friend. When enemies come against your friends and when people say negative things about them, do you shut it down or do you listen to the banter? Although you may not join in on the negative talk, when you do not shut it down, you are being just as bad as the people who are talking. To be a loyal friend you have to shut down the attacks that come against your friends.

2. A Friend is Encouraging

David went into the wilderness to hide from Saul, but he received news that Saul was catching up to him. Jonathan came to David and encouraged him to stay strong in his faith in God. He said, "Don't be afraid. My father will never find you. You are going to be the king of Israel, and I will be next to you, as my father, Saul, is well aware" (1 Samuel 23:17).

We should not only want our friends to have what we have, but we should want them to have *more* than we have. A friend who is not your cheerleader is probably not playing for your team. And if you find it hard to encourage your friends, maybe you are the one who is kicking balls into the enemy's goal. I know you may hate to hear it, but the thing that causes people to have the hardest time encouraging their friends is jealousy. No one ever wants to admit to having jealousy, yet we all have been bitten by the bitter bug of envy. Why don't you want the very best for the friend that you love? Do you believe they don't deserve it or that you deserve it more? Or do you just want what they have?

Being a friend is realizing when God's favor is on your friend and pushing His blessings to come to pass in their life. Discouraging friends can turn joyful experiences into sour moments. It happened to me when I was invited to say my testimony at the New Year's

Rhana A. Gittens

Eve celebration at a church. I was nervous about it, because I had never actually told my testimony before. So when I finally got the courage to do it and completed it, I felt more joyful and closer to God than I had felt in a long time. People I didn't know congratulated me and acknowledged that my testimony was just what they needed to hear to get through their own situations. But when I met with my friends afterword, they started ridiculing me for small things within my speech that they found funny. I was on a high, and it quickly sank. A few weeks later, I thought about that day and began to ask God, "Have I ever made someone feel the way they made me feel? Have I ever been discouraging rather than encouraging? Have I picked on people and told jokes that they may not have found funny?" And the answer to all of those questions was "yes". I realized that in order to have the encouraging friends I so desperately wanted, I needed to be an encouraging friend.

3. Friendship is Bonded by God

Then Jonathan said to David, "May the Lord make us keep our promises to each other for He has witnessed them" (1 Samuel 20:23).

Do you remember the term "pinky swear"? As a kid we whenever you wanted to know you could trust someone with a secret, you tied your pinkies in a knot and made a promise to keep the secret. Regardless of how we create or display our bonds of friendship, God is the final witness of the promise. It can be difficult to keep promises, but when you know you are following in God's will it is your duty to keep your commitments.

Perfectly Loved: Knowing Love on God's Terms

In business, a contract does not have to be written on paper and signed by both parties. It is always more helpful in the court of law to have a written contract; however, verbal affirmations and suggestions are also held up as contracts in court. For Jonathan, his friendship with David was a contract that could never be dissolved without permission from God. When you devout yourself to friendship contracts as you would business contracts, you create a superior reason for being loyal. Although friendship is an at-will contract, meaning either party can leave at any time, when God steps in He provides the ultimate reason to remain loyal. Now you are not loyal because of who the person is but because of who God is.

You remain friends through tough circumstances because you have a contract between yourself, God, and the other person. If God deems for us to remain loyal to a specific person, our love and heart is determined by how we keep that promise. If you are unable to keep the promise or feel that it is not God's Will, you should be inviting and communicate that with your friend. Friendships grow and change as people grow and change. We are never the same as we were at six years old. And by the time you are eighteen, your pinky promise may no longer be sufficient. Indeed, you may grow out of friendship, and that is okay. However, godly friendship proclaims that though you may no longer be best friends with someone, you continue to love that person as you would love yourself. And therefore your pinky promise is never completely dissolved.

Rhana A. Gittens

4. Friends Rejoice in Each Other's Success.

Jonathan was the son of the king and the rightful heir to the throne of Israel, but he knew it was God's will for David to be king over himself. Saul's father swore at Jonathan in a fit of rage, "You stupid son of a whore! Do you think I don't know that you want him to be king in your place, shaming yourself and your mother? As long as the son of Jesse [David] is alive, you'll never be king" (1 Samuel 20:23). Despite his father's reprimanding, Jonathan never stopped endorsing David as the future king.

Gabrielle Douglas, 2013 Olympic gold medalist in gymnastics, had three older siblings—Arielle, a gymnast and ballroom dancer; Jonathan, a football player; and Joyelle, a figure skater. All three of her older siblings let go of their sports so that the family could use any additional money to fund Gabby's gymnastic training[33]. When Gabby won the Olympics, her siblings described how that moment felt like a win for the entire family. They felt like they were out there with her every minute, and they never resented her for being the star she was always born to be[34]. Gabby was blessed to have a family full of Jonathans who would give up their personal dreams in order to fulfill the will that they knew God had over their baby sister's life.

I don't doubt that, that self-sacrifice was extremely difficult for her siblings. There are times when encouraging your friends when they are getting everything you wanted is the most difficult thing in the world. How do you smile as the best man for your best friend's wedding, yet you are still single? What do you do when your football career ended in college because of a torn ACL, but your best friend who never seemed to work as hard as you just got drafted in the second round? How do you hold back the tears when your sister was blessed with three kids, and you just found out that you can't have any?

If all the strangers in the world thought you were the most amazing person that ever lived, it would mean nothing if the people closest to you didn't encourage you. In fact, their discouragement could cause you to fear doing the things that God has called you to for His glory. You never want to be that discouraging footnote in someone else's victory story. Don't be the hater they talk about in their victory speech. Praise and bless others for their successes even when you don't feel like it. The more you show God that you truly want to be a genuine cheerleader for someone, the more He will renew your spirit to be able to cheer without forcing and faking it. Furthermore, if you want to be showered with encouragement, you must show others the love you want to see come out of them. By expressing the love you desire, you receive it in return either from those same people or an unexpected true friend.

Consoling a Friend in Need

While we have discussed the four characteristics that make a friend friendly, there are also friendly habits that we must practice in order to keep genuine relationships. One of those habits is the ability to console your friend when they are in need. The book of Job provides an awesome example of not only God's love but how we can provide love to friends dealing with tragedy.

"How long will you torture me?" Job cried. "How long will you try to crush me with your words? You have already insulted me ten times. You should be ashamed of treating me so badly. Even if I have sinned, that is my concern, not yours. You think you're better than I am, using my humiliation as evidence of my sin" (Job 19:2-7).

These are the words Job poured out to His friends Bildad, Zophar, Eliphaz, and Elihu who attempted to console him during his time of adversity. Job was extremely favored by God because of his high integrity. He had beautiful children, a wife, wealth, and respect within his nation. He was the richest person in the entire area. But most of all, he loved God. God gave Satan permission to test the faith of humans by taking away all Job had and seeing if he would still revere God. He was completely confused by the turn of events in his life, and he cried out to his friends to help him understand why God had let him suffer. God allowed Satan to take Job's wealth, health, and family but not to kill him. Yet Job's three friends Eliphaz, Bildad, and Zophar did not know how to comfort Job in his time of need. This situation provides four key principles in regard to consoling friends and family.

1. Remain silent before speaking

Have you ever had a friend who jumped quickly to speak and give a solution when more than anything you just wanted them to listen? Sometimes we jump to speak and provide solutions before listening or asking God for guidance. If a friend comes to you grieving, first provide a shoulder to cry on. Do not provide words so quickly. Your presence can often be the greatest counselor.

2. Do not attempt to explain reasons for someone's suffering. Rather, just help them endure the suffering.

Unless God has provided you a prophetic wisdom or understanding in regard to your friend's specific situation, you giving numerous scenarios or reasons for their suffering will only add to their grief. Job's friends kept telling him that God placed suffering on him because he had sinned in some way. They persisted in even describing his specific sins. This caused Job to become irritated, as now he felt the need to defend himself and assert his innocence. All tragedy is not necessarily some kind of punishment for sin. And a good friend will not condemn the sorrowful.

3. Pray diligently in the Spirit so that God may provide you the words to help your friend.

Job's fourth friend, Elihu, waited until all the others were done speaking before he presented a comforting response for Job. During his wait, he consulted the Spirit of God to provide him wisdom in answering Job's arguments. Elihu's response created an entry for God to move in Job's life. Although Elihu's answer was incomplete, God was finally welcomed in to complete it.

In the same way, you should fall on your face before God for your friends. You should grieve with them in times of trouble and pray that God provide them an answer through you or some other means. Praying for others opens a blessing in the atmosphere for you. When God finally answered Job, He was very upset with Bildad, Zophar, and Eliphaz for the way they responded to Job's trial. However, God made a way for them and Job to be blessed when He said to them, "My servant Job will pray for you, and I will accept his prayer on your behalf" (Job 42:8), "When Job prayed for his friends the Lord restored his fortunes. In fact the Lord gave him twice as much as before" (Job 42:10).

4. Do not take offense and become abusive when your friend does not agree with you in the midst of his/her anguish.

Whether your consultation to your friend is correct or incorrect, your friend may not accept your response. If he or she does not agree and even seems to become upset with you, do not return their anger with retaliation (Matthew 5:38-39). Rather, continue to provide compassion. If your friend becomes upset with your response, this may be a great time to become silent again and begin to pray in the Spirit for your friend's wisdom, understanding, and peace over their soul.

Selfless Friendship

Many of God's examples of strong friendships in the Bible teach one everlasting principle: selflessness. Through a commitment to selfless friendship and love, the best friends in the Bible were blessed. Our final example of godly friendship comes from the relationship between Ruth and her mother-in-law, Naomi, which is explained in the book of Ruth.

After Ruth's husband died, Ruth stayed loyal to her mother-in-law, Naomi. Naomi told her to leave and go home to her family, but Ruth did not want Naomi to be alone with no family. She vowed, "Don't ask me to leave you and turn back. Wherever you go, I will go, wherever you live, I will live. Your people will be my people, and your God will be my God. Wherever you die, I will die, and there I will be buried. May the Lord punish me severely if I allow anything but death to separate us!" (Ruth 1:16-17)

Ruth's vow was extremely powerful. At the time Ruth made this vow, Naomi had lost her two sons and was going through the hardest time in her life. If Ruth deserted her, she would have been all alone. Like Ruth, we should commit to not leaving our friends, especially when they need us most.

What is striking about Ruth and Naomi's relationship is that all of their differences would have seemingly kept these two from being friends. They were different in age, they were from two different areas, and before Ruth made her vow, they served different gods. After Ruth's husband died, there was no legal connection between the two of them. However, Ruth based her connection with Naomi on a godly bond and promise rather than the legal customs of the time. She understood the eternal love that came with the contract of godly friendship.

Furthermore, this relationship shows that selflessness in friendship goes both ways. Both Ruth and Naomi were willing to sacrifice themselves for the other. Naomi wanted a companion, but she was willing to let Ruth leave her; and Ruth was willing to leave her family back home to be Naomi's companion. We all should be able to lay down what we want most for our friends.

Rhana A. Gittens

God inevitably blessed Naomi with the same companion that she was so willing to let go of. Ruth was blessed also with a motherly friendship from Naomi and later a second husband, Boaz. Naomi taught Ruth how to claim Boaz and helped Ruth know the God of Israel. Their friendship was always in perfect balance. No one person ever gave more love than the other person was able to return.

Although, our digital age can make building strong relationships difficult, in many ways relationships in the digital age have a better chance of lasting forever than ever before. I know this sounds like a total contradiction to my initial analysis of digital aged friendships. However, it isn't a contradiction at all. When used correctly and in tandem with face-to-face and phone communication, digital-age friendships can be successful. Today, we are able to stay in contact with more people than ever before. I am nearing my ten-year reunion for my high school class of five hundred people. It's amazing that I know what 30 percent of my high school class is doing right now simply because of social media. Although we are no longer in the trenches of each other's lives, it's great to be able to congratulate them on the successes they post on social media and encourage them through hard times that they may post as well. In addition, there is little excuse for not contacting family and friends who have moved away. The digital age has made the world so much smaller. My brother and his wife moved from the East Coast of the United States to the West Coast, but we are all able to stay in constant communication and see the growth spurts of my niece by using video conferencing devises. Even more, I'm pretty confident that the well-known theory of "six degrees of separation" may be disproven in this era. The 1960s theory by Stanley Milgram stated that everyone in the world is separated by six links. However, today's theorists claim that social media is shrinking the six degrees. Researchers at Facebook and the University of Milan claim that the degrees of separation between any two people in the world have been reduced to 4.7[35].

We are living in the age of friendship, and friendship is big business. It's not only big business for social media networks and marketing companies; friendship is big business for God. The stronger our relationships are, the more we can share God's love, and the more people we can share the Gospel to. But social networks do not take away the responsibility that is required to be a godly friend.

As we learn to be selfless in our relationships with others and show the love of God in all of our friendships, we will be blessed. Being a good friend is not something that comes overnight. It takes work, just like all relationships take work. We are often quick to call someone else a bad friend, but we should also analyze what kind of friend we are being. After reading this, you now know how to be a friend in God's way, but there will be people in your life who do not follow these principles. It does not necessarily mean they are bad friends. Everyone will make mistakes, and it is our job to love them through their mistakes. However, God has blessed us with a Spirit of discernment that provides the wisdom to know when to let someone go and how to deal with difficult relationships. Our next chapter will discuss some of those principles as God proclaims them in the Bible.

Rhana A. Gittens

Think About It

1. Who is your best friend? Use the characteristics of Jonathan, David, Job, Job's four friends, Ruth, and Naomi to describe why this person is your best friend.

___

2. Now turn it on to yourself. Use one of the characteristics of Jonathan, David, Job, Job's four friends, Ruth, and Naomi to analyze an aspect of friendship that you may not be living.

___

3. For the aspects of friendship that you are not currently living, describe ways you can change that.

___

Perfectly Loved: Knowing Love on God's Terms

_____

_____

_____

MY STORY - NATALIE

I was broken. I was in a relationship with highs and lows. Somewhere along the way I got lost in the lows. I lost connections with my friends, with myself, and with my God. But the crazy part is I was angrier with myself than I was with him. I forgave him quickly and fully for all he ever did, but I couldn't forgive myself. I had let another human come before everything else and break my soul. He showed me his true colors more than once, and I allowed myself to get hurt over and over. He took advantage of my forgiveness because he knew I would accept him unconditionally.

I felt like I was allowing someone to take my kindness for weakness. Forgiveness has always been something that comes naturally to me. I was angry at myself, because I wished I wasn't like that; I wished I was stronger so people wouldn't step all over me. Loving others has always been easy to me. But in the midst of loving hard, I forgot to love myself. In my inability to forgive myself, I was becoming a reflection of the person and people who were hurting me.

But thank God, He surrounded me with people who forgave me for me, who loved me for me, who accepted my flaws, and even now are helping me accept my own flaws and find the person I once was—the person God wants me to be. I realize now your imperfections are good for the hearts that are meant to love you. Even more, I realize this feeling of love that resonates in me and causes me to forgive others and love unconditionally is God within me. I don't have to feel bad for loving. I found peace in being able to receive love through God from others and share that. I am able to forgive others because I see the good God put in them and I choose to love them rather than focus on the negative. After I forgive someone, I feel closer to God. I know that it is what He would want and expect of me. In forgiving others, I feel a weight lifted off my shoulders. It is so much harder to live life mad and resentful. In forgiving, I open myself to receive love and forgiveness in return.

And I don't forgive because my kindness is my weakness but rather because my kindness is my greatest strength and my purpose. I choose to forgive, because I choose to trust in the Lord.

Chapter Ten

Love Forgives

Study Verse – *"Bless those who persecute you. Don't curse them; pray that God will bless them. Be happy with those who are happy, and weep with those who weep. Live in harmony with each other. Don't be too proud to enjoy the company of ordinary people. And don't think you know it all!" Romans 12:14-16*

On November 23, 2012, Michael Dunn pulled into a gas station in Jacksonville, Florida. He parked next to a red SUV full of teenagers playing loud music. Dunn expressed to the teens that he was upset with the loud music and exchanged words with passenger, Jordan Davis. In his fierce anger, Dunn opened fire on the car of teens, killing Davis. The adolescents in the vehicle were unarmed. Dunn went on trial, and on February 15, 2014, he was found guilty of three counts of attempted second-degree murder on the other injured passengers, but the jury could not reach a verdict on the first-degree murder charge of Jordan Davis[36].

Ta-Nehisi Coates, national correspondent at *The Atlantic*, met with the mother of Jordan Davis, Lucia McBath, after the trial.

Rhana A. Gittens

Below is an excerpt from the February 25, 2014, article he wrote about their conversation (written in Coates's first person)[37].

> "I told her that I was stunned by her grace after the verdict. I told her the verdict greatly angered me. I told her that the idea that someone on that jury thought it plausible there was a gun in the car baffled me. I told her it was appalling to consider the upshot of the verdict—had Michael Dunn simply stopped shooting and only fired the shots that killed Jordan Davis, he might be free today.
>
> She said, 'It baffles our mind too. Don't think that we aren't angry. Don't think that I am not angry. Forgiving Michael Dunn doesn't negate what I'm feeling and my anger. And I am allowed to feel that way. But more than that I have a responsibility to God to walk the path He's laid. In spite of my anger, and my fear that we won't get the verdict that we want, I am still called by the God I serve to walk this out.'"

I consider Lucia McBath a hero. She reconciled in her heart that regardless of the verdict, she would forgive the killer of her seventeen-year-old son. She is a hero of the Kingdom of God because she showed love in spite of anger to a man that no human being would blame her for hating. It is because of acts of love like McBath's that Jesus came off that rugged cross and rose with all power for the salvation of sinners. I imagine that every time we choose not to forgive or love in the midst of difficult relationships, we nail Jesus right back to the cross.

Perfectly Loved: Knowing Love on God's Terms

Throughout all of our lives we will be faced with difficult relationships and times where our love for God is tested by our obedience to his demand of us to love others. Furthermore, not only will we face difficult times in loving enemies, but we will be challenged with deciding when to end close relationships or when to continue to love close friends and family despite the circumstances. Human beings will never completely live up to our expectations, and there are many actions we can take when these difficult situations arise. In this chapter we will first discuss how to deal with difficult relationships and choosing when it is time to let someone walk out of our lives. We will end this chapter with the very important concept of forgiveness.

Letting a Friend Go

Loving people can be confusing at times, especially when loving that someone means we have to let them go. It seems counterintuitive to the whole concept of loyalty and unconditional love. However, there will be times when God tell us that to truly love someone we have to leave someone, and He has multiple reasons for doing it. Sometimes we cannot move into the next step in our purpose with that person, and other times they cannot take us with them on the next step in their purpose. For whatever reason, our close proximity with someone may need to end. Nevertheless, love for that person is never demolished.

The story of Lot and Abram in Genesis 13:8-14 provides a great example of choosing when to let a friend go.

God promised Abram (Abraham) that he would be blessed with a nation but that he would have to leave his native country, his relatives, and his father's family and go to a land God had shown Him. Abram partially did what God instructed. He left his native country with his wife, but he also brought his nephew Lot along with him when God distinctly told him to leave his relatives at home. Both Abram and Lot had their own flocks of sheep. The land that Abram went into could not support both of their flocks living close together. Lot's and Abram's herdsmen began to argue over the land. In order to stop the conflict, Abram told Lot to choose whatever section of the land he wanted and they would separate. Lot chose the land of Sodom because it was the best land, but it was in a city known for its sin.

Abram and Lot separated because they were arguing over land. If they had stayed together, Lot would have been blessed with the territory God gave to Abram. However, through the bickering and jealousy, Abram finally allowed Lot to leave.

This event exemplifies two important principles of God's love:

1. When God first tells you to let someone go, do it.

Abram was never supposed to bring Lot with him, but he did anyway. We need to understand that God is protecting us when he tells us to let someone go. Be aware of God's first command to you and follow it completely. Because Abram chose to keep Lot, he had to deal with the consequences.

2. If someone wants to leave, let them.

Jesus warned His disciples when they went to share God's healing gifts that, "If any household or town refuses to welcome you or listen to your message, shake its dust from your feet as you leave" (Matthew 10:14). We must do the same thing.

God does not force Himself into our lives. He asks us to invite Him in, and once invited He comes. Therefore, who are we to force people to stay in our lives if they don't want to be there? Abram was to be blessed with all of the land, and Lot would have been blessed as well if he had stayed. However, Lot did not see the blessing that was upon Abram and decided to leave. So, too, there are people in our lives who do not see the miraculous gifts and destiny that God has in store for us. If they do not see our value or want to be a part of our value, they may ask to leave. And when they ask to leave, we let them. Shaking the dust off of your feet signifies that it is their loss and not ours. The Apostle John writes, "They left us, but they were never really with us. If they had been, they would have stuck it out with us, loyal to the end. In leaving, they showed their true colors, showed they never did belong" (1 John 2:19 MSG).

I have been in what I thought was love with the wrong guys many times, and my hurt came when I tried to force people to be with me who didn't want to be there. They had other things they wanted to do. Whether they didn't want to settle down or they wanted to date other women didn't matter. The fact was that they wanted to leave me, and it was not my job to force them to stay.

When someone wants you to back off, do just that. They will soon see the blessing they lost just as Lot inevitably saw when God destroyed the city of Sodom and Gomorra (Genesis 19:16).

Rhana A. Gittens

Loving In Spite Of...

"Loving in spite of" is simply forgiving. You must love in spite of ANYTHING, EVERYTHING, and NOTHING AT ALL.

"You'll never know how strong your heart is until you know how to forgive who broke it!" said Christian life coach and speaker Kimberly Pothier[38].

But what exactly is forgiveness? People say "I forgive you" a lot, but do they really? What does forgiveness feel like? The problem is that forgiveness isn't a feeling at all. It is an action. In the midst of deciding to forgive someone, you may still feel angry, but you make a conscious decision to disregard your anger and act in love. When you forgive, you let go of any vengeful thoughts that may inhabit your heart, and you decide to let go of bitterness. But forgiveness does not mean that you forget. The events really did happen, and you will need to take some action toward keeping them from happening in the future. Forgiveness doesn't excuse wrong behaviors. Rather, it allows you to continue to treat the person with kindness despite their actions.

We often judge ourselves by our intentions and judge others by their actions. You say if you didn't intend to hurt anyone's feelings then how they take it is their problem. When the situation is in reverse, we don't always feel the same way. It's easy to be mad at a person's actions when you don't take the time to understand their heart. Being able to forgive often requires us to look at our own flaws and realize that in the same way that we mess up, other people mess up as well. We forgive others because there will be a time and has been a time when we needed to be forgiven.

Don't always think of forgiveness as a gift to the person who hurt you. To a large extent, forgiving someone is a gift for you. It keeps you from harboring anger, resentment, and bitterness. Those feelings, untamed, can turn into hate, which can cause you to take actions you never expected. The Oxygen Network show "Snapped," which chronicles real life stories of wives who commit murder primarily to their spouses, is no joke. These women who could have once lived lives of innocence and love were pushed to their limits; rather than forgiving, they allowed hatred to consume them and turn into violence. Many of these women never expected to be that person, and they may even plead a moment of insanity because they and their family would say, "She is just not that type of person. She would never do that." But untamed anger can bring out the darkest parts of you that you never wanted to release. You may watch those shows and think it could never happen to you, but keep letting your hatred fester and you will see how vicious you could become. God calls us to love and forgive so that we never have to see the vicious sides of our flesh.

In addition, the act of forgiving gives you the power back. It frees you from a burden that could be the cause of other problems in your life such as inability to trust, communicate truthfully, or be vulnerable in certain situations. Forgiveness is a gift for yourself, and it frees your heart to love unconditionally.

Abram's relationship with Lot also exemplifies the act of forgiveness. Abram chose to solve the problem and end the behavior that was causing their arguments by letting Lot go. But Abram never stopped loving his nephew. Even though Lot left, Abram was there for him during his desperate time of need. Soon after Lot moved, the rebel kings of Sodom and Gomorrah battled in the Dead Sea. The armies of Sodom and Gomorrah fled, and the victorious invaders plundered Sodom and Gomorrah and captured Lot and took everything he owned. When Abram heard about this, he mobilized his men and pursued the rebels and recovered all of the goods that had been taken and brought back Lot with his possessions (Genesis 14: 8-16).

Though people leave us, we should never stop loving them. We are often quick to become vindictive and vengeful when someone leaves us. We do it because of the emotional hurt and scar that they have left behind, and we often want them to feel that as well. We declare that we will never answer the phone for them again or "one day they will need me and I won't be there." However, we now know that God's love is not provoked and suffers through hardships. When you love the way God intended, you may suffer heartache, but do not be provoked into a vengeful spirit. Your love for someone else should endure *in spite of.* God's love does not state that you love them if they love you. Rather, you love them whether they like you or not. In fact, you might not even like them very much anymore. But you are still called to love them. If the people who walk out on you call you a week, month, or years later asking for help and you can help, you must help if God tells you too. We have turned our backs on God so many times. But every time we invite Him back into our lives, He comes. In the same way, we should love others as God has loved us.

Perfectly Loved: Knowing Love on God's Terms

Sometimes when people hurt us we want to see them hurt too. Our consciences tell us not to wish bad on anyone. And though you may not physically wish that bad things would to happen to them, we have all had times when we just watched and waited for someone to fail so that we could say, "I told you so." When I was in college, I made a point to never post my relationship status because I knew others would be excited about my loss of relationships. I could point out that characteristic in others because it lived within me. I had a bad habit of going on Facebook and being excited when I saw someone's status go from "in a relationship" to "single." God checked my heart on that, though, and helped me realize how horrible having an excitement about someone else's loss really was. I had to remove myself from social media for a time in order to get my own spiritual walk together.

It is easy for you to love others when you are able to truthfully acknowledge the flaws in yourself. Do not think of yourself more highly than anyone else. When we find ourselves pointing out other people's flaws so clearly, it is often because we harbor those same flaws in ourselves. We just commit our sins in more socially acceptable ways[39]. For example, when you notice the sin of gossip in someone else, it is important to ask yourself if you portray gossip in any way as well. Paul says in Romans 2:1, "You may think you can condemn such people, but you are just as bad, and you have no excuse! When you say they are wicked and should be punished, you are condemning yourself, for you who judge others do these very same things."

We should never be happy in someone else's sadness, whether or not we feel that they deserve it. God does not want us to be that way. He said that He would make our enemies our footstool (Psalm 110:1), but He did not say we should pray that they fall. Through love we should always pray that God has mercy on the people who hurt us, because we know our God will get vengeance and His vengeance isn't pretty. So when we are praying for God to have mercy, we are praying God forgive our enemies as He has forgiven us for mistakes we have made. And we pray that they have a repentant heart, that God may forgive them for all their transgressions against us.

Pray for your enemies...

It is so important to pray for your enemies and people you may not like. I made a point to list the people who hurt, betrayed, and became my enemies, and started to pray for them. I prayed for them every day. In the beginning it was so difficult for me to say nice things or pray that God bless them. The prayers started off really short. Before I would go to sleep I would just say, "Lord, Bless 'em". I often kept reliving the moment they offended me and feeling like they didn't deserve my prayers. My pride started to get in the way. But the more I did it the easier it became. Soon I started saying their names, "Lord, Bless X,Y, and Z". Then, I had to start praying to God to give me the pure heart I needed to be able to pray for them. As time went on I realized that I loved these people and I really did want the best for them. God was changing my heart through my prayer for them. He was even helping me to forgive them. After a while I wasn't just saying meaningless words any more. I became more passionate about God having mercy over them and blessing them to walk in His Will. I now want them to have all the blessings God has given me. This change in my heart proved that the Word of God will change your spirit and the more you pray the Word of God over other people's lives the more that love comes to dwell in you.

I understand how hard it is to pray for people you do not like. It seemed so difficult for me to insert someone I didn't likes name into a prayer of blessing. But I just kept forcing myself and moving my fleshly pride out of the way. I had to defeat my flesh. And when I couldn't defeat my flesh, I would pray for them in my heavenly tongues. My Spirit man was becoming so strong and wanted to pray for them. This taught me that if I am having a hard time praying for someone I need to let my Spirit do the work.

I finally was able to defeat my flesh and I grew to love these people and I had to remove them from enemies list because I want so much good to happen to them now. I was surprised at how God changed my heart for these people who I use to curse at night. Now I pray for God to have mercy on them and strengthen them to do His Will and walk in His way.

Prayer inevitably leads to reconciliation. Reconciliation occurs when you are able to speak to the person that offended you, settle your differences, and live in harmony. If you were once close friends with this person, that closeness may never return. However, reconciliation allows you to clear the air so that there is no divisiveness' between you. Furthermore, praying for our supposed enemies helps us to put into perspective who our real enemy is.

Paul reminds us in Ephesians 6:12 that "we are not fighting against flesh-and-blood enemies, but against evil rulers and authorities of the unseen world, against mighty powers in this dark world, and against evil spirits in the heavenly places."

What's so amazing about living in love is that when you do, God makes your enemies live in peace with you (Proverbs 16:7). When you live in love, you disarm your opposition[40]. It's difficult for a mean person to be mean to a loving person. Granted, there are exceptions to this rule, but your kindness often blocks enemies from acting out against you. In fact, your kindness causes other people to stick up for you when your enemies do plot against you. One of my good friends told me about a girl who hated me, but I never knew she hated me. I talked to this girl all the time and never knew she didn't like me. My friend told me that he said to the girl, "How could you hate Rhana? She is nice to everybody." Because of my reputation as a kind person, she would look crazy if she had ever tried to attack me. The people who knew my reputation would immediately jump to my defense. If you create a reputation of love, you cause your enemies to back down from the plans they have to harm you. They realize that no judge would believe the lies they may say against you, because your record of love disarms the enemy.

Remember, our brothers and sisters in Christ are not our enemies. Of course, they annoy us sometimes just like any brothers and sisters do, but we must understand that we are working toward the same goal, the Great Commission (Matthew 28:16-20). We are waging the same war. We shouldn't be turning our guns on each other. Even if the person you have an out with is not a Christian, we must still understand the same principle. The reason why they are not a Christian is because of the evil principalities that seek to keep them from hearing, understanding, and believing the Good News. Therefore, we do not seek to destroy them but to love them. We seek to bring them to Christ and share the good news with them.

Lucia McBath had every reason in the world to hate Michael Dunn, the killer of her son. But even Michael Dunn is a fleshly body acting out the will of the devil. Michael Dunn is not the enemy. The devil is, and Satan would love to see hate rage in Lucia's heart to the point that she retaliated against Dunn. But God allows these situations to occur in order to show His love to the world. In forgiving Michael Dunn, Lucia is showing humanity how God's love works, and she is showing love to Michael Dunn that could possibly free him from his evil habits. McBath states, "In spite of my anger and my fear that we won't get the verdict that we want, I am still called by the God I serve to walk this out." You too were called to walk out in love. Don't let your unforgiveness be the nails that put Jesus to the cross.

Think About It

1. **Read -"Bless those who persecute you. Don't curse them; pray that God will bless them. Be happy with those who are happy, and weep with those who weep. Live in harmony with each other. Don't be too proud to**

enjoy the company of ordinary people. And don't think you know it all!" – Romans 12:14-16

2. **Now Declare It. Put your name in the blanks.**

_____ will bless those who persecute him or her. _____ will not curse them. _____ will pray that God bless them. _____ will rejoice with those who are happy and cry with those who are sad. _____ will live in harmony with everyone. _____ will not be too proud to enjoy the company of ordinary people. And _____ will not think he or she knows it all.

3. **Make a list of people from your past or present that you do not like, consider as your enemies, or have offended you.**

   a. _____
   b. _____
   c. _____
   d. _____
   e. _____

4. **Write a prayer of blessing for them.**

_____
_____
_____
_____
_____

Perfectly Loved: Knowing Love on God's Terms

MY STORY -LATASHA

"Why should I have two bowls of cereal when I only need one and there is someone out there who doesn't have any bowls of cereal?" I said.

"What if someone in your family needs one later?" my best friend said after I told her my plans.

"But what if someone I don't even know needs one right now, but they don't have it?" I responded.

I think about how the majority of the world's people are complete strangers to me. I know less than .000000001 percent of the world's population, but I was called to love every single one of them. And there is someone out there who needs my love. Jesus sacrificed His perfect body for us all. In no way am I Jesus, but He called us all to serve. The sacrifice He made for us makes it easier to sacrifice things for others.

So sacrifice is what I'll do. I have decided to donate a kidney. I've literally had to start treating my body like something I am giving away to somebody else. I have to change my diet to make sure my kidney is perfect for this stranger. I have to think about the fact that I'm going to be off work for four to six weeks during recovery and money will be unsure in that period. Not everyone will understand, but nothing has made me second-guess my decision thus far. Donating a kidney isn't something everyone is meant to do.

I have fought against serving so much. I have felt worn and drained from sacrificing. But that worn-out feeling only comes when I'm trying to do stuff without my source. God is my source. Me without God has no ability to serve, sacrifice, and care the way I was created to. I am going through this new sacrifice with Him.

"The human contribution is the essential ingredient. It is only in giving of oneself to others that we truly live." That is a quote by Ethel Percy Andrus, the first woman high school principal in California. It is also the signature line in my email. It reminds me to ask myself, "Who am I to think I can live without serving?" God gave us all key gifts, and every gift can and is meant to be used for someone else. It's crazy, because I've had times where I have purposefully fought against my gift of service. But it was more work for me to fight against it than it was to just do it.

So now I'm just doing it. And it's rewarding. It makes me cry with joy just thinking about it. I may never meet the person who gets my kidney. I may never hear their voice or know their name. But I will never forget them. I hope that they may know God loves them and this gift would never be possible without Him.

Chapter Eleven
Love Serves

Study Verse – *"Your attitude should be the same as that of Jesus Christ: Who, being in very nature God, did not consider equality with God something to be grasped, but made himself nothing, taking the very nature of a servant, being made in human likeness. And being found in appearance as a man, he humbled himself and became obedient to death – even on a cross!"*

Philippians 2:5-8 (NIV)

On Martin Luther King Jr. Day 2013, I volunteered at a men's shelter in Atlanta that teaches Christian values. That day, a team of volunteers and I helped beautify the shelter by cleaning up the garden area, assisting in painting the dormitories, and scrubbing clean the cafeteria. We also made sandwiches for lunch. During lunch time the shelter opens up for the residents and the homeless in the city. There were about 150 men who come in on MLK Day to eat. The majority of the volunteers were women. A lot of these men don't get hugs or conversation with women on a regular basis, so we all took the time to chat with them and hear their stories. I spoke with one gentleman for about fifteen minutes during lunch. He talked about how he had graduated college, traveled the world, and at one point was making six figures. He told me that in the midst of all the traveling, he didn't spend much time with his wife and kids, and eventually his wife left him. He started drinking, and his alcoholism led him to losing his career. He became homeless, but then he found the Christian shelter, and they were helping him get back on his feet. After I spoke with him, I started to make my rounds to network with the other men. I was so excited to be serving them. When lunch was over, they all said bye to us in what seemed to be an unusual way to me. They said, "God bless you. I will be praying for you." I was so confused, because I was sure I was the one who should be praying for them, but somehow the tables had turned. I was no longer the one doing the serving for people I considered "needy." Instead, they were now serving me by sharing their thankfulness with love.

I will confess to having what I call the "Suburban Syndrome." I move to the suburbs, drive to my nice little job every morning, go to church, hang out at nice restaurants in nice neighborhoods, and suddenly forget the world outside of the suburbs. I grew up in the inner city of Florida, but like many people who "make it out," I forgot where I came from. Volunteering and being with people in need reminds me that the world is not this comfortable little box that I put my life in. I was called to not just get myself out but to free others as well. It makes me cry to see people hurting. It makes my heart broken to see people with closed eyes to God. It's becoming a burden for me to see children living homeless or in abusive homes. It just doesn't seem fair for me to live well and them to live hurting when they are so innocent. My heart is growing for others. I am beginning to feel other's pain, and this helps me to love others how God loves me. It is bringing me back to the realness of the world I am in and how the devil destroys lives. Sometimes we can get so spiritual that we are no earthly good. But our godly spirits are on this earth for a mission. We can't forget the job God gave us. We may not be of this world, but we are definitely in it. We are His warriors on the ground. The battle is won in heaven, but through the Spirit in us, we bring that victory to fruition on earth.

I taught you earlier that love is an action. In fact, love is the only required action that God gave us in regards to our relationships with other people. We don't owe anyone anything but to love them. The problem for humans is that in loving others, other requirements become attached. If loving others means going out of my way to do something for them, then I must do it because it is required.

God gave us the Holy Spirit to make loving others easy for us. If we allow the Spirit to guide our thoughts and actions toward people, we are able to fulfill God's requirement of love. We know that we are living by the Spirit when we see the fruit of the Spirit growing in our lives and the lives of those who we interact with. The fruit of the Spirit is love, joy, peace, patience, kindness, goodness, faithfulness, gentleness, and self-control (Galatians 5:22-23). We are able to produce this fruit when we remain in communion and closeness with God. Through our vertical relationship with Him, the Holy Spirit transforms us to be more

Christ-like, thereby producing the heavenly fruit. This is what it means to be the fruit of the vine (John 15:5).

In Philippians 2:5-11 (NIV) Paul writes, "Your attitude should be the same as that of Jesus Christ: Who, being in very nature God, <u>did not consider equality with God something to be grasped</u>, but <u>made himself nothing</u>, taking the very <u>nature of a servant</u>, being made in human likeness. And being found in appearance as a man, he <u>humbled himself</u> and <u>became obedient to death</u>—even on a cross! Therefore, God exalted him to the highest place gave him the name that is above every name, that at the name of Jesus every knee should bow in heaven and on earth and under earth, and every tongue confess that Jesus Christ, is Lord to the glory of God the Father."

In order to serve we must embody the traits of Jesus Christ. In psychology courses they teach the concept of "reciprocity." This concept basically states that if you do something good for someone, they normally reciprocate that with another good. Psychologists argue that people don't give and volunteer simply because they are selfless but because they have something else to gain from altruism. Psychologist Mark Snyder PHD, University of Minnesota, argues that there is an egoistic component to all altruism, and people gain something for themselves either by reciprocity of another or some personal desire[41].

However, if you are truly a Christian and Christ-like, then Snyder's argument is absolutely false. If you consider yourself to be serving with the underlined characteristics based in Philippians 2:5-11, then you are serving as Christ did and there is no personal gain or reciprocity that motivates you. God wants all of us to serve others out of selfless love for Him and for others. In order to do that, we must learn what characteristics of service in love God is calling us to.

First, you must not consider yourself equal with God or attempt to be equal with God. Yes, you are called to be Christ-like or "little Christ." However, you are not Christ. You are not God. In comparison to God, you are nothing. Without God, you are absolutely nothing. And without you, God is everything and can still do everything. Knowing these truths should not make you feel worthless. Rather, it should make you feel powerful in the thought that you serve the God that is so great that no one can ever be His equal. Your goal in life is to strive to live as He did as Christ but to understand that you can never be Him.

Once you understand that you cannot be equal with God, you then realize that you must be His servant. As a human, you serve God on the earth and you bring about His plans for human beings by doing as He requests. You serve someone so great and mighty that when your Father in heaven asks you to love others, you do it simply because He said so and because He is your God.

Next, you must humble yourself not only to God but to other people. You are not to think of yourself as better than anyone else. You are not worse than them, but you are not better either. Just as God made you for a specific purpose with specific gifts, He made everyone else with the same thing and the same option to follow Him. You are no better than anyone because you follow Him, nor are you better than anyone because of your gifts. All gifts are necessary for the Kingdom of God, and they do not work in isolation. Rather, they work together in order to help others and glorify the Kingdom of God.

Whenever you start to think of yourself as greater than anyone else, start to ask yourself questions that will remind you to be humble. If you have the gift of prophecy, ask yourself, what is the purpose of my ability to speak God's plan if there is no one with the gift of administration to put God's plan to action? What is the purpose of my gift to speak in tongues if there is no one available to interpret what I am saying? What is the purpose of my gift to heal if there is no one with the gift of mercy to accept the healed back into the community? And what is the purpose of my life if God did not give it to me?

Furthermore, as humble servants of God we are obedient to love to the point of possible death. If God told you that in order for you to live eternally you must die in order to save someone else, would you do it? It all sounds so extreme, but it is so real, and it is the final epitome of love. By death God does not necessarily mean a death physically; rather, He speaks of a death to yourself and to your flesh. Are you capable of giving up all the things you want in order to help someone else? Love is the purest form of self-sacrifice and may actually call the person who is presenting love to be uncomfortable.

Love sounds so good. It's such a beautiful term, and we love to say it to people. We love to boast about being in love and how much we love our friends and family. However, when we love others by serving them, we may just have to sacrifice something else we love for them. Some of those sacrifices are as simple as waking up two hours early to take someone to the airport for an early flight. Others may be a little trickier. What if you saved up for five years and were ready to put down the deposit on the house of your dreams, but your parents call and tell you they don't have money to send your little brother to college? Would you give up your savings for him?

Can you think of the things that you love the most in life and imagine giving that thing up for the sake of someone else? Sacrificing your best and greatest for someone else is the purest level of love and the love that God presented to us when Jesus died on the cross for our lives.

Before Jesus went to the cross, He sat with His disciples for a final supper (John 13:1-17). At the final supper, Jesus got up from the table, took off his robe, and filled a basin with water, and began washing the disciples' feet. The disciple Peter protested, "No, you will never ever wash my feet." Peter could not understand why His Lord would stoop to wash His servant's feet. Jesus said to the disciples, "You call me 'Teacher' and 'Lord,' and you are right because that's what I am. And since I, your Lord and Teacher, have washed your feet, you ought to wash each other's feet. I have given you an example to follow. Do as I have done to you. I tell you the truth, slaves are not greater than their master. Nor is the messenger more important than the one who sends the message. Now that you know these things, God will bless you for doing them."

Rhana A. Gittens

When Jesus washes the disciples' feet prior to going to the Cross, He is being an example of love through humble service that He wants them to portray to the whole world after He leaves. While we will never be equal to Jesus, in His human flesh Jesus successfully exemplified the need for serving. Jesus took off His robe and slowly transformed Himself into looking like a servant or a slave, and then He washed the disciples' feet.

In the same way, Jesus wants us to take off our refineries such as the nice suit of a man going to his white-collar job or the evening gown of a young lady headed to a gala. He wants you to remove all the outer signs that cause you to be presented as greater than others and humble yourself to be able to serve and sacrifice for them. How can we make this practical to our lives? For me, I can take off the vision of my dress suit and blazer, glass-view corporate office, 12:00 p.m. lunches, and go out in my community. I can serve the people who work on the manufacturing line to sew my garments, wash the glass windows of my corporate office, and clean the tables at my favorite lunch tavern. I can serve them and give honor to their work by taking extra time to speak to them when I see them, give them an extra tip at the lunch table, and help them carry the bucket of water and glass cleaner. It's as easy as acknowledging the janitor at your school or office and asking them how their day is going, rather than walking past them as if they are invisible. I must stop to realize that the things that I have do not just appear out of nowhere. Rather, I am able to live the "Suburban Syndrome" because someone else has served me with their gifts. I would have nothing without someone else's humble service to me and in the same way I can utilize the blessings God has given me to bless them in return. In that way I am no greater than them and they are no greater than me. We are all utilizing the gifts God has given us to serve each other.

When Jesus served His disciples He was not only giving them an example of what humility looks like, but He was giving them a view of what God's love really is. Serving others is how we show people the way God loves us.

In order to build Christianity we must be real Christians. Being real Christians requires us to be Christ like. The Holy Spirit gives us a chance to be real Christians by building up the fruits of love, kindness, and faith within us. Christians should weep at the thought that people doubt God's love. After Jesus' crucifixion, He was buried in a tomb. On the third day, He rose from the tomb and He came back to the disciples before leaving to go back to heaven. However, the disciple Thomas doubted that He was really Jesus when He came to Him from the grave. In order for doubting Thomas to believe, Jesus had to show him His hands that had been punctured by the nails during the crucifixion (John 20:24-29). There are many people that doubt that Jesus is alive. They are nonbelievers. In order for them to believe, we have to show them Jesus' hands. We have to show them the hands that serve, the hands that love, the hands that sacrifice for them. People have to see God's love in order to believe in God's love. And how can they believe without someone to show them? You were sent to show them.

Rhana A. Gittens

Think About It

1. List three of your most prized possessions, some things you worked really hard for or have a high value to you.

    a. _____

    b. _____

    c. _____

2. How can you serve someone else by giving away your most prized possessions?

   _____
   _____
   _____
   _____

3. List three talents, abilities, or gifts that God has blessed you with.

    a. _____

    b. _____

    c. _____

4. How can you use these three gifts to serve other people?

_____
_____
_____

5. In what ways can you serve the people who have served you?

_____
_____
_____

MY STORY - MATTHEW

I am well aware of the fact that I am a mess.

That's my first and truest revelation. But despite my messiness, there were various sources that showed me God's love growing up and inevitably led to my salvation. There is one particular man who always comes to mind. This guy really showed me what a Christian was and what being a man was. He did that by showing me imperfection. I know he didn't purposefully show me his flaws, but he just lived life right in front of me. Having a Christian man there, hand-and-hand, walking beside me, and being real, has always stuck with me.

That experience revealed to me that the world is missing authenticity. I feel like today's Christian does not love people often and does not love people well. A lot of people are at odds with each other and with God because they don't have a manifestation

Rhana A. Gittens

of love in their life. Christians are supposed to be that manifestation. When you listen to music and watch television, everybody is talking about things they don't have. It seems like no one is real. If people in the church could be the realness, we could do something. I don't want to put on another face for the sake of sharing the Bible. I want the gospel to be shared through this real life that I am living.

I had a coworker who was an atheist one day, a pantheist the next day, and a pseudo Christian on another day. Most of his upbringing was anti-Christian. Another Christian coworker in the company was extremely combative with the guy. He would tell him, "You're wrong. I don't want to listen to what you have to say." When I saw this happening, I decided I needed to treat this guy differently. I wanted to show him that I was listening. One day my non-believing coworker said to me, "I really appreciate that you listen to me. When I talk to you, it doesn't feel like you are trying to beat me." After speaking with him and hearing what he had to say, I realized we actually had something in common. We were both broken people. Suddenly I did not think I was better than him; the playing field was level. That's where I found compassion. When I thought I was better than him because I was Christian, I actually had pity on him. But pity has no power. My pity wasn't going to bring him any closer to God than he already was. My compassion would. I realize I may not be the one who ultimately gets him saved, but I don't think that's my job either. My role is to love him.

Perfectly Loved: Knowing Love on God's Terms

Since this encounter, I have started to change my music. When I was young and just getting into rapping, my music was different. I can listen back to those songs and hear how it comes across as if I'm talking from this plateau that the listener has to get to. Now I want my music to express to people that we are in the same fight together, and I just have this one key difference that is going to help me win and this one thing can help the listener win too. That one thing is God's love.

I know sharing God's love, being real, and bringing people to Christ is not easy. It's my very real imperfections that make it feel even harder. But all that doesn't matter when love is the single command. I might not always see the outcome of the love I've shown, but God has given me a gift of patience that helps me through that. I wait patiently on God. I'm not just sitting down, but I'm being still. We may want all of our friends and family to be saved and we seek God for it, but when we talk to them we don't show them love and we don't show them God. When you pray and then do your due diligence to show love, well, then you're being still in God knowing that by faith your love will make the difference in someone else's life.

Rhana A. Gittens

Chapter Twelve
Loving Others to Christ

Study Verse - *"Look our Lord, this town is well situated, but the water is bad and the land is unproductive. ' Bring me a new bowl,' Elisha said, 'and put salt in it'. Then he went out to the spring and threw the salt into it saying, "This is what the Lord says, 'I have healed this water. Never again will it cause death or make the land unproductive.'" 2 Kings 2:19-22 (NIV)*

A young man had a dream. He woke up in a beautiful glass house. There were specialty rooms for him to do everything he loved. He had a sporting room, a gaming room, a reading room, an eating room, a fishing room, an extreme sports room, and a pool room. The ceiling was made of glass. Through it he could see when the sun came out and when the sun went down, but somehow it never got dark. Every morning there was a plate of his favorite breakfast at the front door—a veggie omelet with pancakes and bacon. When he got tired of that meal, his breakfast plan changed without him ever saying a thing. The tables shimmered and the floor glowed. The couches and bed were cozier than the

Perfectly Loved: Knowing Love on God's Terms

Westin Excelsior in Rome. The furniture was European Medieval style with gothic touches. It reminded him of his childhood trips to the medieval fairs with his dad.

In the sporting room he could announce whatever sport he wanted to play, and the room would change at his whim. For the first few days he played basketball and practiced some free throws. He was so excited. By day three he decided he wanted to fence. He remembered fencing with his dad in the backyard. So he went into the sporting room and announced "fence." The scene changed to a fencing ring. He was suddenly wearing a white, cotton fencing jacket, a plastron, knickers, and mask. And a fencing sabre flew into his gloved hand. Suddenly he realized there was no one else there for him to play with. He announced, "Dad, Dad," thinking maybe his dad would appear like everything else did. But nothing happened.

Then he started running around the house to see if there may be another room that his family was in. "Family room," perhaps. He found nothing. He looked out every window and saw nothing. He ran out the door for the very first time since he'd been there. Outside there seemed to be a complete dome surrounding his home, and far off in the distance were all the people he ever knew and loved. He ran toward them, forgetting the glass dome and hitting his head. He screamed and banged to get their attention, but they heard nothing. They were all walking outside the dome. They looked extremely worn, pale, and thin. His little sister looked like she hadn't eaten in days. He kept banging because he saw his mother crying. But he couldn't get to them.

***

There will come a day when Jesus comes back to earth to get all the people who believed. He will sweep us off to heaven, and we will be adorned with the beauty of His many mansions. That good news is for all of us who believe, but what about those who don't believe? What about all the people who we say we love so dearly but have never shared this gift with? How can you say you love someone and not share this gift? The true confirmation of your love for your family and friends will be shown in your exuberant effort to share the love of Christ with them so that they can share in the heavenly mansion with you. What good is your Salvation if you are the only one who makes it in? The young man's dream is a warning to all that believe. The true Heaven will be absolutely amazing for believers and we will not feel lonely for a minute because we will be with God in heaven. But this young man's dream is simply a warning to be concerned for the salvation of those you love so that they too can experience the wonders of heaven.

Paul says in Acts 20:24, "But my life is worth nothing to me unless I use it for finishing the work assigned me by the Lord Jesus—the work of telling others the Good News about the wonderful grace of God."

We, the body of Christ, are the salt of the earth. The love that dwells within us makes unproductive places new. Love brings life back. We are in places that look good on the outside but are unproductive and dying on the inside. We meet people every day who look good on the outside but are devoid of love on the inside. They lack the Spirit of God and, therefore, also lack the Spirit of love. However, like the prophet Elisha used the salt to heal the water, God wants to use you to heal the people you are connected with. There are networks that you have made that your pastors, evangelists, teachers, and ministers will never be connected to. There are gifts God graced you with that are specifically being formed and grown in you to bring someone else to the knowledge of Christ. No man should have to wait for a pastor or minister to hear about the Word of Christ. It is the job of the entire body of Christ (each of us believers) to fill the springs of water with our salt and, thereby, fill the empty places of people's hearts with God's love.

So far we have learned how to define godly love, remove hindrances from receiving and giving the gift of love, and develop and act on the gift of love. One of my favorite pastors once taught me that the Litmus Test for perfecting your love is the result of the changes of your heart. The more God's love grows in your heart, the more Christ-like you become, and the more your heart will be set on the desires of God. And what was Christ's final desire and mission that He gave His followers? The answer is "The Great Commission."

"The Great Commission" is the spreading of the Good News to everyone. The Good News is the gospel of Jesus Christ. Jesus says to the disciples in Matthew 16:19, "Therefore, go and

Rhana A. Gittens

make disciples of all the nations, baptizing them in the name of the Father and the Son and the Holy Spirit. Teach these new disciples to obey all the commands I have given you. And be sure of this: I am with you always, even to the end of the age."

The more perfect our love becomes, the more we desire to pray for others, do charity, and spread the gospel. Jesus's burdens become our burdens. His goals become our goals. As God makes our hearts more like Christ's, hurt souls become a burden on us just as they were a burden on Jesus.

In this chapter, I will not be providing a step-by-step instruction manual on how to make disciples, evangelize, and bring others to Christ. This book is about the growth of the gift of love in us. This chapter is set to encourage you to take those next steps in your godly gifts and loving *all* people to Christ despite our worldly predispositions of who may and may not be worthy of God's love. This study begins with the greatest of all missionaries: Paul.

Paul was treacherous.

If you didn't know Paul's story before reading this, you may not have expected that to be the first thought of our greatest missionary. But it's absolutely true. After Christ's death and ascension to heaven, Peter and the other disciples first began spreading the Good News to the Jews. But Paul (known as Saul before His conversion) was out persecuting and taking believers of Christ as prisoners. This is the same guy who wrote thirteen books of the New Testament. The same guy who is today one of the most fervent apostles and teachers in the Christian walk that we study.

This same guy was out there trying to stop the spreading of

the gospel by any means necessary. But the story of Paul's conversion (Acts 9:1-17) is one of God's greatest examples of love and demonstrates beyond a shadow of any believers doubt that God can and will choose anyone to be His and use anyone to do His work.

The gift of love in our hearts teaches us to look at others with non-judgmental eyes. To look at people not as we see them but as God sees them: God sees us all as children He loves and cherishes.

Paul says in 1 Corinthians 2:14, "People who aren't spiritual can't receive these truths from God's Spirit. It all sounds foolish to them and they can't understand it, for only those who are spiritual can understand what the Spirit means." We must pray that God open the hearts and eyes of nonbelievers as He did for Paul. It is difficult to explain simple concepts to nonbelievers, because their eyes have not been opened. Explaining forgiveness to a person who is not led by your same Spirit can feel like talking to a brick wall. But the good news is that God can unveil His Word to those He chooses. It's not our job to choose whose eyes are opened. Our job is simply to tell everyone about the eye-opening power of God. God will choose whose hearts will be softened to salvation.

Aranias, the believer who was called to minister the Gospel to Paul (known as Saul at the time), had to give up his personal beliefs about Saul being a treacherous nonbeliever. He had to give up what he knew Saul to be so that Saul could be what God called him to be (Acts 9:10-17). That's what loving others to Christ is all about. It's about looking past who they are without God and looking toward who they can be with God. We often look at derelicts, drug addicts, criminals, and even people we don't like, and we shun them. We may decide that it's not worth our time to minister the Gospel to them because they will just turn away. But through the example of Paul, God is expressing that you do not turn from ministering the Gospel to anyone. The Gospel must be preached to the entire world. God called us to love those people. Jesus died to save the lowliest of sinners and the poorest of people. He died to take the lowest of this time and make them the highest. He died to take the weak and make them strong. He died to take the poor and make them rich, the uneducated to make them wise. He died to take the unloved and show them love. But all of this is done through each one of us who has the love of Christ dwelling within us.

Bringing others to Christ is not quantified as a success by how many successful conversions you have had, how many disciples you have made, or how many times someone can directly attribute their salvation to something you did. We plant seeds, and it is God who waters them. We find success in doing the will of God and not in our own glory. It is God who converts people to Christ. There will be times when we don't see the full fruit of the seeds of love we have planted in someone because God uses someone else to water those seeds. Your mission is not to count but to *do*. When I really got into writing this book and truly believed in it, I started to get worried that no one would get anything from it, or even more, maybe no one would read it. But God revealed to me that if only one person reads this book and that one person grows in a new level of Christ-like maturity through the seed of this book, then every word written was worth it even if that one person was just me.

"What do you think? If a man has a hundred sheep, and one of them goes astray, does he not leave the ninety-nine and go to the mountains to seek the one that is straying? And if he should find it, assuredly, I say to you, He rejoices more over that sheep then over the 99 that did not go astray." (Matthew 18:12-13 NKJV)

God loves each of us so much that when He sees us go astray, He runs after us and rejoices when we return to Him. He rejoices more for the new member of the Kingdom than for the ninety-nine who were already saved. When one of His children is saved, the angels in heaven rejoice (Luke 15:10). Therefore, there is no need to count your acquisitions and seeds of love that were planted. In fact, there should be no record kept. As God gets all the glory and your competition against man to gain ninety-nine believers means nothing to God if He only called you to get one. It's all about what God has called you to on an individual level. Therefore, we do not compete in the body of Christ. Each one is granted with his own gift and own purpose, and each is as significant as the other. The pastor who is working in his purpose is just as significant as the church janitor who is working in his purpose, because both are needed in the Kingdom of God.

Furthermore, as you love other people to Christ, it is important that you continue to not be judgmental and you do not cause them to stumble. It's even more important that you become aware that you are an example of Christ in all you do. In taking on the burdens of Christ, there will be some sacrifices you have to make in your own character and daily actions in order to keep new believers and even seasoned believers from stumbling. All of these sacrifices are acts of love in themselves and based in the following scripture from Romans 14:

"Accept other believers who are weak in faith, and don't argue with them about what they think is right or wrong. For instance, one person believes it's all right to eat anything. But another believer with a sensitive conscience will eat only vegetables.... Who are you to condemn someone else's servant?... So let's stop condemning each other. Decide instead to live in such a way that you will not cause another believer to stumble and fall… But if you have doubts about whether or not you should eat something, you are sinning if you go ahead and do it. For you are not following your convictions. If you do anything you believe is not right, you are sinning" (Romans 14:1-2, 4, 13, 23).

Believers at all levels may ask questions such as, "Is it okay to go the club?" "Can I drink alcohol?" "Can I eat red meat?" "Can I listen to secular music?" There is no rule against such things in the New Testament. But even more, as Christ followers, following specific laws to the 'T' is not how we perfect the law within ourselves. The lesson to learn from the above Scripture is that God changes your heart, and as you grow in perfect love, you will discern what you should and should not do. Even more, when you begin to walk with God and realize specific destinies God has for your life and sins you are attempting to free yourself of, you will find that going to the club, drinking alcohol, or listening to secular music may cause you to stumble into sin. These things have different effects on different people. Therefore, if your friend tells you that they do not drink or they do not go to the club, you should never pressure them to do it. In addition, you should not do those things in front of them, because you may cause your friend to stumble into sin. For example, if you have a friend who does not listen to secular music and they ask you for a ride, you start bumping all the secular music you can think of. You are better off riding in silence. You do not know the temptation that may cause your friend to stumble and separate them from their walk with God. In loving people to Christ, you choose to abstain from all things that could cause your brother or sister in Christ to stumble and revert to their sinful nature. Someone once asked me why I stopped listening to sexual slow jams. I said, "I'm not having sex, so why should I tempt myself with the excitement of other people having it?" I had to let go of that music in order to remain pure in my vow of abstinence.

As followers of Christ, we do not live our lives based on tradition and rules. Christ did not come to give us religion, but He came to give us relationship. Through our personal relationships, He will guide us away from things that will cause us to fall out of relationship with Him. But He will guide each believer in His own way and His own timing. I teach this lesson because I believe it is one of the most significant aspects of loving people to Christ, and not knowing this aspect could cause the people you are loving to backslide.

Rhana A. Gittens

Now that you are hopefully more encouraged to use the love God has built up inside of you to bring others to Christ, it is time to evaluate your current actions and determine ways that you and your local church family, as well as the entire body of Christ, can become more effective in loving people to Christ.

Think About It

1. **Romans 1:14-15 (NIV) says, *"I am obligated both to Greeks and non-Greeks, both to the wise and the foolish. That is why I am so eager to preach the gospel also to you who are in Rome."***

    Personalize Romans 1:14-15 by adding your name to it.

    _____ (your name) is obligated both to believers and nonbelievers, both to wise and the foolish, to the civilized and the un-civilized. _____ is eager to spread the gospel to all.

2. **Now take both the original scripture and the personalized scripture and paraphrase it again. Think about the people you have not shared the gospel with and name them specifically. Think of the groups of people who may need the Word of Christ and name those groups specifically. Continue to personalize it with your own name.**

    _____
    _____

Perfectly Loved: Knowing Love on God's Terms

_____

_____

3. Read - Acts 2:42-47; Acts 4:34

Acts 2:47 *"And the Lord added to their number daily those who were being saved."*

The believers of the first church after Jesus died and was resurrected were bringing new believers daily to God. There were specific characteristics of the first believers that allowed them to bring people to Christ in the droves that they did despite the horrendous opposition they faced. Acts 2:42-47 explains those characteristics, and I have listed them below. Examine yourself first and foremost. After each of these characteristics, give yourself a score between 1 and 5, 1 being that you never exhibit these characteristics and 5 being that you exhibit these characteristics daily. Then, in the second column evaluate your local church family. In the third column, evaluate how you feel the entire body of Christ is doing based on what you can see.

Perfectly Loved: Knowing Love on God's Terms

CHARACTERISTIC	YOUR SELF	YOUR CHURCH	THE BODY OF CHRIST
1. Perform spiritual miracles and/or support those who exhibit gifts of healing, prophesying, tongues, interpretation of tongues, discernment, etc.			
2. Fellowship with other believers.			
3. Giving away your possessions and goods to the needy			
4. Selling your possession and goods to give offering or giving tithe and offering out of your salary.			
5. Meeting with other believers in Church as often as the Church is open for such activities.			

Perfectly Loved: Knowing Love on God's Terms

6. Being glad in the successes of believers and the coming of new believers with a sincere heart.			
7. Devoting yourself to learning God's Word by reading His Word daily.			
8. Praising God daily.			

4. How can you become stronger in characteristics where you scored yourself a 3 or less?

_____
_____
_____
_____
_____

5. How can you build up your local church family to become stronger in the characteristics where they scored 3 or less?

_____
_____
_____

Rhana A. Gittens

6. How can the actions you do on a personal level and the actions your local church do affect the effectiveness of the Body of Christ?

The entire world is waiting for Christians to live like Christians. When we start acting in love as the first church did and giving our lives to handle God's work of spreading the Gospel to the entire world, we will see more people saved. But before we can get other people to believe that God is real, we must start living our lives as an exemplification that God is real. Who is going to believe the Word we share if the carriers of the Word don't live it themselves and show its truth through their lives?

"The reason the world does not know us is because it did not know Him" (1 John 3:1). Therefore, you, as a Christian, will never be accepted and understood by the people of this world who do not know your Father. In knowing this, we must teach the world about Him so they may come to understand the love and joy we have through Him" (1 John 4:6).

Perfectly Loved: Knowing Love on God's Terms

Loving others to Christ and serving others in love is the fruit of our salvation. It is possible to think you are in a relationship with God when you are not. The Apostle John writes in 1 John 2:4, "If someone claims, 'I know God,' but doesn't obey God's commandments, that person is a liar and is not living in the truth." This verse is not a test of God's love for us but a test of our love for God. Our love for God is exemplified in the actions we take daily and the way we treat others. If we truly love God, then we obey all of His commands. "How do you act when you are "in love" with a significant other? You speak to them every chance you get, you make sacrifices for them, you think of them before you think of yourself, you talk about them with everyone, and more. If you will do all those things for a human being you are in love with, how much more would you do for the God who had His son die for you to show you how much He loves you?

You can share the gospel to others by simply sharing your story. Every chapter in this book included a testimony from people just like you and I. When these love stories are shared, people learn the realness of God from your experiences. We all have our own love stories that remind us of God's love for us. Could you imagine that everything you went through in your life was simply so that your story could save someone else? But what if you don't share your story? That would make everything you went through worthless. Christians often keep what they have in Christ to themselves. They show it off to people by wearing a cross or posting statuses about God's favor on their lives, but their actions often show that they don't want to share God with others. Do you hold onto your story and your lessons for yourself? There is enough of God to go around to everyone. I understand why you may not want to share a piece of cake. I mean, you can't eat your cake and have it too. But the most amazing thing about God is that you can share Him and have Him all to yourself at the very same time.

Service and spreading the Good News through love are just action steps of the growth of love in you.

If I'm going to die, I'm going to die standing up for Christ. Is what you're living for worth dying for?

Conclusion

God's Love isn't something that comes by happenstance or chance. It's not a roll of a dice. The odds are always in your favor with God's love.

Love always is and always will be. It was here before time, and it will be here after we cease to exist. Whether or not we open our hearts to know and share love is on us. It's given to everyone—freely, forgivingly, and forever.

Love is so misunderstood it's crazy. Love wants you to just believe that it is, that it's true, and that it's everlasting.

God's love is perfect. You don't have to search for perfect love. The epitome of His love is already flawless. It's staring right back at you saying I'm here, I'm real, I love you, I love you perfectly. Please take this statement with you forever. *You are perfectly loved.*

Bibliography

[1] *Live Real: Where Religion and Science Meet Common Sense.* (n.d.). Retrieved June 28, 2014, from Why Are We Here? The Live Real Quiz: http://www.livereal.com/spiritual_arena/why_are_we_here.htm

[2] Fleming, V., & Cukor, G. (Directors). (1939). *The Wizard of Oz* [Motion Picture]

[3] McKay, V. M. (Composer). (2008). The Corinthian Song. [M. Stampley, Performer] On *Ransomed*. Infinity Entertainment Group and Music World Music.

[4] *Merriam-Webster.com*. (2013). Retrieved January 2, 2013, from http://merriam-webster.com/dictionary/fear

[5] Tribbett, T. (Composer). (2013). If He Did it Before... Same God. [T. Tribbett, Performer] On *Greater Than*. T. Tribbett.

[6] MacDonald, W. (1995). *Believer's Bible Commentary.* Nashville, TN, US: Thomas Nelson Publishers, Inc.

[7] Stone III, C. (Director). (2002). *Drumline* [Motion Picture].

[8] Sontag, D. (2010, January 17). Amid Rubble, Seeking a Refuge in Faith. *The New York Times*. Port-Au-Prince, Haiti. Retrieved 2014, from nytimes.com: http://www.nytimes.com/2010/01/18/world/americas/18church.html?_r=0

[9] Strong, J. (1990). *The New Strong's Exhaustive Concordance of the Bible.* Nashville, TN, US: Thomas Nelson Publishers.

[10] Strong, J. (1990). *The New Strong's Exhaustive Concordance of the Bible.* Nashville, TN, US: Thomas Nelson Publishers.

[11] Strong, J. (1990). *The New Strong's Exhaustive Concordance of the Bible.* Nashville, TN, US: Thomas Nelson Publishers.

[12] Abbott, E. (Producer), & Marshall, P. (Director). (1996). *The Preacher's Wife* [Motion Picture].

[13] MacDonald, W. (1995). *Believer's Bible Commentary.* Nashville, TN, US: Thomas Nelson Publishers, Inc.

[14] MacDonald, W. (1995). *Believer's Bible Commentary.* Nashville, TN, US: Thomas Nelson Publishers, Inc.

[15] *Life Application Study Bible* (2 ed.). (2007). Carol Stream, Illinois, US: Tyndale House Publishers, Inc.

[16] *Firefly*. (2013). Retrieved February, from Firefly.org: http://www.firefly.org/facts-about-fireflies.html

[17] Warren, R. (2002). *The Purpose Driven Life*. Grand Rapids, Michigan, US: Zondervan.

[18] Warren, R. (2002). *The Purpose Driven Life*. Grand Rapids, Michigan, US: Zondervan.

[19] Moceanu, D. (1997). *Domonique Moceanu An American Champion*. Yearling.

[20] Warren, R. (2002). *The Purpose Driven Life*. Grand Rapids, Michigan, US: Zondervan.

[21] Copen, C. E., Daniels, K., Vespa, J., & Mosher, a. W. (2009, March 22). First Marriages in the United States: Data From the 2006–2010 National Survey of Family Growth. *National Health Statistics Report*(49). Retrieved from http://www.cdc.gov/nchs/data/nhsr/nhsr049.pdf

[22] Martin, J. A., Hamilton, B. E., Osterman, M. J., Curtin, S. C., & Mathews, a. T. (2013, December 30). Births: Final Data for 2012. *National Vital Statistics Report, 62*(9). US Department of Health and Human Services Center for Desease Control and Prevention. Retrieved from http://www.cdc.gov/nchs/data/nvsr/nvsr62_09.pdf

[23] Amato, P. R. (2005). The Impact of Family Formation Change on the Cognitive, Social, and Emotional Well-Being of the Next Generation . *Marriage and Wellbeing, 15*(2).

[24] Amato, P. R. (2005). The Impact of Family Formation Change on the Cognitive, Social, and Emotional Well-Being of the Next Generation. *Marriage and Wellbeing, 15*(2).

[25] Amato, P. R. (2005). The Impact of Family Formation Change on the Cognitive, Social, and Emotional Well-Being of the Next Generation. *Marriage and Wellbeing, 15*(2).

[26] Amato, P. R. (2005). The Impact of Family Formation Change on the Cognitive, Social, and Emotional Well-Being of the Next Generation. *Marriage and Wellbeing, 15*(2).

[27] Williams, H. A. (n.d.). Freedom's Story Teaching African American Literature and History. *Freedom's Story, Teacher Serve*. National Humanities Center. Retrieved March 2014, from National Humanities Center: http://nationalhumanitiescenter.org/tserve/freedom/1609-1865/essays/aafamilies.htm

[28] Bevere, J. (2004). *The Bait of Satan: Living Free From the Deadly Trap of Offense*. Lake Mary, FL, US: Charisma House.

[29] Bevere, J. (2004). *The Bait of Satan: Living Free From the Deadly Trap of Offense*. Lake Mary, FL, US: Charisma House.

[30] *Child Sexual Abuse by the Numbers.* (n.d.). Retrieved March 2014, from National Center for Disease Control and Prevention: http://ncdsv.org/images/ChildSexualAbuseByTheNumbers.pdf

[31] Smith, A. (2014, February 3). *6 New Facts About Facebook.* Retrieved from Pew Research Center: http://www.pewresearch.org/fact-tank/2014/02/03/6-new-facts-about-facebook/

[32] Harkness, Elder C. (2014, February 16). Sermon Message: Love is Loyal. *Destiny Metropolitan Worship Church.* Marietta, GA.

[33] Champion, G. (Director). (2014). *The Gabby Douglas Story* [Motion Picture].

[34] Winfrey, O. (Producer). (2012). *Oprah's Next Chapter: Gabrielle Douglas: First Family Interview* [Motion Picture].

[35] Backstrom, L. (2011, November 21). *Anatomy of Facebook.* Retrieved 25 March, 2014, from Facebook.com: http://www.facebook.com/notes/facebook-data-team/anatomy-of-facebook/10150388519243859

[36] Sanchez, R. (2014, February 16). *Florida 'loud-music' murder trial's verdict evokes mixed reactions*. Retrieved April 3, 2014, from CNN.com: http://www.cnn.com/2014/02/15/justice/florida-loud-music-trial-reaction/

[37] Coates, T.-N. (2014, February 25). *'I Am Still Called by the God I Serve to Walk This Out'*. Retrieved April 3, 2014, from The Atlantic: http://www.theatlantic.com/politics/archive/2014/02/i-am-still-called-by-the-god-i-serve-to-walk-this-out/284064/

[38] Pothier, K. J. (2013, September 22). *RealTalkKim*. Retrieved from Twitter.com/RealTalkKim: https://twitter.com/RealTalkKim/status/381925958040961024

[39] *Life Application Study Bible* (2 ed.). (2007). Carol Stream, Illinois, US: Tyndale House Publishers, Inc.

[40] MacDonald, W. (1995). *Believer's Bible Commentary*. Nashville, TN, US: Thomas Nelson Publishers, Inc.

[41] Winerman, L. (2006, December). Helping Others, Helping Themselves. *American Psychology Association, 37*(11). Retrieved from American Psychology Association: http://www.apa.org/monitor/dec06/helping.aspx

CPSIA information can be obtained at www.ICGtesting.com
Printed in the USA
LVOW10s1006290116

472416LV00019B/296/P